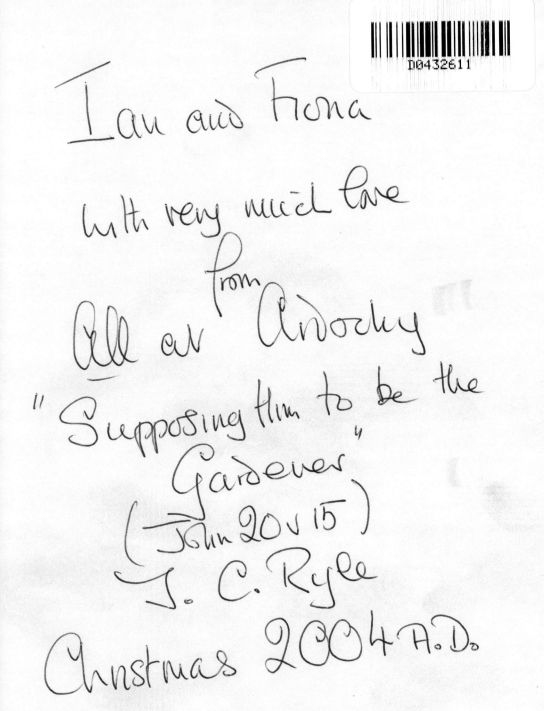

Ian and Fiona

with very much love

from

All at Ardochy

"Supposing Him to be the Gardener"

(John 20 v 15)

J. C. Ryle

Christmas 2004 A.D.

'Glory be to God for dappled things.'
Gerard Manley Hopkins

Mother of Pearl
original painting *by Katharine Woolmer*

John and Jane Woolmer have been married for over 30 years. John was a teacher of Mathematics at Winchester College. It was here that he rediscovered a childhood interest in butterflies. After a clear call to ordination (reluctantly received), John stayed on as a school chaplain before moving to Oxford where he was first curate at St Aldate's and then priest in charge of St Matthew's. For nearly twenty years, he was Rector of Shepton Mallet with Doulting and Cranmore in Somerset. He became involved in overseas mission – mainly to Zambia where the diocese of Bath and Wells has a strong link. In 2002, he moved to Leicester to join the staff of Holy Trinity Church, and to work as a Springboard Missioner. He is currently in charge of a 'church plant' which meets in various pubs in NW Leicester, and works with ReSource (Anglican Renewal Ministries).

Jane did a short photographic course before reading economic and politics. She married John in 1974 and they have four grown up children. She teaches economics, loves horse-riding, and sometimes accompanies John on his overseas missions. With great patience, she taught an exceedingly impractical husband how to wield a camera (while he showed her how to find butterflies!). They have had photographs published in many books, calendars and magazines. They have contributed articles for the Sunday Times, the Arusha National Park official guide, Kenya airways and Brittany Ferries.

About the Photographs

The photographs were taken with a Nikon FE2 camera body, Nikon 105mm macro lens (plus extension rings when appropriate) and flash unit. For many years, they have used Fujichrome film (50 ASA, 35mm transparencies). Most of the photographs were taken in natural situations (except for the emergence sequences), a few were taken using 'capture and release' (see chapter 6 for instance). The best times for photography are in the early morning when butterflies are opening their wings in order to absorb heat so that they can fly, when they are feeding, laying eggs, distracted by the delights of courtship, or in the early evening when they are preparing to rest for the night.

Their most effective work is when John discovers the butterflies, eggs, caterpillars or chrysalises, and Jane does the photography!

Acknowledgements

The book was designed by Lion Hudson plc. The authors are enormously grateful for their unfailing courtesy, patience, and design skill. The publishers, the Word for Life Trust, have given helpful and enthusiastic direction. WFLT do much mission work, prayer ministry, counselling and training in UK and overseas (especially in India where they have developed a number of social and theological projects).

The Grand Surprise

Butterflies

and the Kingdom of God

Text   John Woolmer
Photographs   John & Jane Woolmer

Word for Life Trust

Published by Word for Life Trust, the House of Bread, Ross Road,
Christchurch, Glos GL16 7NS. All enquiries to the publishers e-mail wflt@wflt.org,
or the authors at Fig Tree Cottage, Hallgates, Cropston, Leicester LE7 7GQ.
E-mail jwoolmer@onetel.net.uk.

ISBN: 1 903577 49 7

Distributed by:
New Wine Ministries, 22 Arun Business Park, Bognor Regis PO22 9SX
Email: newwine@xalt.co.uk

British Library Cataloguing Data
A catalogue record for this book is available
from the British Library.

Book design by Lion Hudson plc, Mayfield House,
256 Banbury Road, Oxford OX2 7DH.
Printed in Singapore.

Contents

Dedicated to our children Rachel, Susie,
Tim and Katy who follow Jesus and who
have accepted with good humour
their Father's hobby and have appreciated
their Mother's photographic skill.
With grateful thanks to Oxford Scientific
Films, Karl Bailey and Robert Goodden
for their encouragement, help and advice
and to the design team at Lion Hudson.

Apologia

Apprehend God in all things, for God is in all things.
Every single creature is full of God, and is a book about God
Every creature is a word of God.
If I spent enough time with the tiniest creature – even a caterpillar
I would never have to prepare a sermon. So full of God is every
creature.

Meister Eckhart (1260–1327)

For nearly thirty years, I have wanted to write a book which would attempt to combine my calling as a Christian with my love of butterflies, and my wife Jane's photographic skill.

Jesus used nature as the basis for many parables (for instance, the sower, the wheat and the tares, and the mustard seed). He used the natural beauty of flowers to teach about anxiety: 'Consider the lilies of the field, how they grow; they toil not; neither do they spin. And yet I say unto you, that even Solomon in all his glory was not arrayed like one of these' (Matthew 6:28b–29, AV). Thus it seems legitimate for the Christian writer or preacher to contrast the quintessentially selfish lifestyle of the caterpillar with the gloriously responsible

Photo 1: A nest of Small Tortoiseshell caterpillars (caterpillars 9mm). Several hundred caterpillars are clustered together for their mutual protection. Later on, they live in smaller groups. They continue to feed on nettles until they disperse to pupate. Small Tortoiseshell females like to lay their eggs on young tender nettles growing in full sunlight. Patches of uncut nettles under trees left by lazy gardeners will attract neither Small Tortoiseshells nor Peacocks. Photo x3

freedom of the adult butterfly. It seems appropriate to look at an empty chrysalis case, and then to revisit the observations of St John about the empty tomb (John 20:1–10). These analogies will be familiar to many readers.

Other 'parables' included in this text, as far as I am aware, have not yet been used by preachers. It seemed right to link the Mourning Cloak (the name given in USA, Germany and Scandinavia to our Camberwell Beauty – which was named long ago, more romantically, as the *Grand Surprise*) with the pain and darkness of bereavement. There was a moment of quiet revelation when I noticed that the glorious under wings of the majestic Poplar Admiral contrasted dramatically with its sombre upper wings, which are opened only when the butterfly basks in the sun. There is a parallel to be found pastorally in the lives of many people who can look quite beautiful and serene, until the pain of their past is opened up by the Sun of Righteousness 'risen with healing in his wings' (see 'Hark! the herald angels sing' which is based on Malachi 4:2). As the reader will discover, there are many other examples which spring from the natural history of our butterflies and which, from this fresh perspective, can teach us old familiar truths.

Amateur natural historians frequently enthuse about the beauty of butterflies, and many see their gratuitous beauty as signs pointing to the hand of a gracious creator. Professional entomologists often look at the same insects with great wonder but also display deep scepticism about any form of divine creation. Atheistic evolutionary theory seems easily proved. The existence of such terrible enemies of butterflies, such as ichneumon flies, tends to confirm many in their disbelief. The sheer impossibility that a benign creator could allow such desperate battles at every stage of the butterfly's life-cycle can be a huge obstacle to belief.

Christians, and other seekers after truth, will not find 'proofs' in this book, any more than Jesus proved the truth of his teaching in his parables. Proof, in so far as it is possible, comes from examining the evidence for the signs of the kingdom (in a small way I have tackled this in other books).

The serious natural historian will very properly regard this

Photo 2: A Small Tortoiseshell (wingspan 52mm) photographed shortly after emergence (indicated by the vivid colouring especially in the blue spots at the edges of the wings), feeding from the flowers of a thistle. Small Tortoiseshells have two, or even three, generations each year. Many hibernate in houses or churches. Ideally, they need to be in a cold place – without central heating!
Photo x2

book as a frivolous diversion from the rigorous pursuit of scientific truth; equally some Christians may be uneasy at my openness to theories such as mimicry which are probably best explained in evolutionary terms. This small book is not really intended to be read at that sort of level. It would be better to enjoy it as a mosaic of information about butterflies, from which some kingdom thoughts may be drawn. The parables of Jesus usually only made one point. Over-interpretation of details tends to lead to theological chaos. If our butterfly pictures and parables make even one point, something may have been achieved. If not, then enjoy the photography (shared by Jane who taught a severely impractical husband to wield a camera and with grateful thanks to George Bernard of Oxford Scientific Films who spent a memorable hour giving us a life-time of instruction). Butterflies have livened up many of my sermons, especially at baptisms and funerals, and have helped in evangelism. This in turn has led to several life-long friendships, and caused some amusement to my Zambian friends, who have named me the chimpimpele (butterfly) man. The sight of a visiting preacher lying on a dusty road, prostrate in front of a pile of dung, photographing butterflies did wonders for cross-cultural relationships!

... for he commanded
and they were created

Psalm 148:5

CHAPTER
1

Through the Year with a Swallowtail

(Conversion)

"And we'll live, and pray, and sing, and tell old tales,
and laugh at gilded butterflies."
(*King Lear*, Act 5, Scene3)

Photo 1: Swallowtail (wingspan 75mm, natural size) photographed feeding in southern France. The British Swallowtail is featured at the end of the chapter. The swallowtail is easy to see in most of Europe, and has up to three generations in the south. Many eggs are laid on fennel on roadside verges.

The gilded butterflies, which bring a glimmer of light and laughter to the poor mad king at the end of his tragic reign, offer us hope and provide us with a wonderful parable of the Christian life. Mankind has always needed hope, perhaps now as never before.

Our world floats on a sea of pessimism; much of it justified. A few years after the dawn of the new millennium, we live in a planet which seems to be full of wars, terrorism, natural disasters, the destruction of rain forests, unjust trading policies and diseases like AIDS; while future generations seem likely to face environmental disasters caused by global

warming, air pollution, water shortage, and the inbred selfishness of man.

Such negative sentiments are as old as time. Listen to the Old Testament writer of Ecclesiastes:

'Meaningless! Meaningless!' says the Teacher. 'Utterly meaningless! Everything is meaningless. What does man gain from all his labour at which he toils under the sun? Generations come and generations go, but the earth remains for ever.'

(Ecclesiastes 1:2–3)

In the seventeenth century, the philosopher Thomas Hobbes described the life of man as 'solitary, poor, nasty, brutish, and short.' Similarly, in the twentieth century, the French existentialist writer Jean-Paul Sartre wrote that 'Man is condemned to be free' and that 'Man is a useless passion'. Rudyard Kipling, writer and poet at the beginning of the last century, offers a little light relief:

The toad beneath the harrow knows
Exactly where each tooth-point goes;
The butterfly upon the road
Preaches contentment to that toad.

(Pagett M.P.)

Can the butterfly, that most fragile, frequently endangered insect offer us more than *contentment* – perhaps even a parable of hope? Can the butterfly, often used as a symbol of an after-life on gravestones, flash its iridescent wings and point us away from ourselves, and show us the way back to our creator?

I believe so: but first a few brief memories. It was a beautiful spring day, the flowers were blooming in a Parisian park, Jane and I were looking after Katharine our youngest child, then just three months old, and with our English hosts enjoying a quiet picnic. A newly emerged Swallowtail swooped out of the sunlit sky, circled around us, descended, and while basking on a warm bare patch of earth, opened its freshly coloured wings. We enjoyed his presence for a full minute, then with a quick flick of his wings, he soared off high into the azure blue sky. Even the troubled Lear might have raised a smile. On the same trip, we were inspired by the colours of the Impressionist painters in their magnificent new gallery, but struggling with Katharine amidst the artistic throng. Suddenly, a gallant Frenchman doffed his hat, bowed and pointing to Katharine, said, 'She is far more beautiful than any of the paintings.' A sentiment with which Shakespeare's deeply pessimistic Jaques, as will become clear later in the chapter, would not have agreed!

In France in 1996, I was enjoying part of a period of sabbatical leave at Valbourges, south of Draguigan. Here Helene, a family friend, oversees a lovely old rambling estate which makes quality wine and yet leaves plenty of woodland and rough ground for wildlife. I spent four weeks writing, walking and praying in the private chapel – a place of mystic quiet beside the ancient gatehouse of the leafy courtyard. Walking carefully amidst the long grasses (a few days earlier a wild boar and I had eyed each other with mutual suspicion), I noticed that the Swallowtails had started to lay their large yellow spherical eggs on the wild fennel plants. In much of Europe, Swallowtails are common. They have many breeding plants, including carrots to the annoyance of some farmers. As I had plenty of time left in France, I decided to farm a few of the eggs. Over the course of the next seven weeks, I was able to observe the full life cycle of the butterfly.

Photos 2–4:
Swallowtail eggs and emergence of a caterpillar (height of the egg is 0.9mm).

2   3   4

By contrast, the British Swallowtail is a very rare and particular butterfly. Its life cycle usually lasts a full year. Today, it can only be found in a small area of fenland in the Norfolk Broads. It breeds on milk parsley, a flowering plant that grows

Photos A–F: Members of the wider Swallowtail family which are found in East Africa. Christmas or Citrus Swallowtail (wingspan 110mm); Central Emperor Swallowtail (wingspan 120mm); Horniman's Swallowtail (wingspan 110mm); Small Striped Swordtail (wingspan 90mm); White Banded Swallowtail (wingspan 80mm); Angolan White Lady (hind-wing 40mm). Worldwide, the larger family called the Papilionidae numbers about 500, and includes the largest and most beautiful of the world's butterflies (see chapter 8). In Europe, there are only four different species of Swallowtail – two of whom can easily be seen. There are also seven members of the larger family (the Festoons and the Apollos).

amidst the reed beds which flourish near the rivers and streams of that part of the country. This behaviour is totally different from its continental cousin. The European Swallowtail has a varied habitat. I have seen Swallowtails, in Europe, in mountainous areas, on rough ground beside roads and railways, as well as in the marshy surrounds required by their British cousins. The most likely reason for this is that the British Swallowtail can only just survive in our colder climate, and has adapted quite differently from its continental relative. In England, there is often only one generation of butterflies (see below); in southern Europe there will be two or even three.

If you visit the River Ant, or one of a number of other similar rivers on the Norfolk Broads, in late May or early June, you may be rewarded by seeing courting swallowtails flying high over the reed beds. Their spectacular, highflying mating ritual is one of the great sights for any naturalist. Eventually they descend to the reed bed, pair, and then the female searches for suitable plants on which to lay her large yellow eggs. This she does with immense care, skimming just above the vegetation to lay them either on prominent milk parsley plants, or on ones that have been recently mown by the keepers of the fens. The egg stage lasts just over a week; in this time the egg darkens, and the small caterpillar can clearly be seen inside the shell. When it emerges, the tiny caterpillar resembles a bird dropping. Unfortunately this doesn't fool the resident spiders, and it is estimated that up to two thirds perish before their first skin change.

Photos 5–7: First three stages of swallowtail caterpillar (natural size 7mm, 15mm, 22mm). Note the dramatic change in the colouration of the caterpillar through successive skin changes.

5   6   7

The caterpillar passes through five stages, moulting four times, eventually being transformed into a large handsome green caterpillar, marked with black, and armed with two curious defences. Like other members of the genus, it has a strange orange coloured scented organ, called an osmeterium, which enables it to produce a pungent scent, a little like crushed pineapple, and a small V-shaped structure which looks like a snake's tongue. Nevertheless despite these defences, many fall victim to predators – mainly reed buntings, sedge warblers and bearded tits. Perhaps only a fifth of the original egg population, of about a hundred, will reach the next stage – pupation. The surviving caterpillars leave their food plant, (which is as well to remember if you are ever keeping these caterpillars in captivity!) and climb up a convenient reed.

Photos 8–11: Fourth (including the old larval skin which the caterpillar then ate!) and fifth stages (natural sizes 30mm, 35mm, 41mm), also the caterpillar preparing to pupate.

8

9

10

11

Here they spin a girdle and, after being motionless for perhaps two days, the transformation begins. The skin splits, and gradually the pupa forces away the old larval skin and emerges, attached to a reed by the girdle that the caterpillar had spun, and by a silk pad at its base. The pupa is coloured green or brown (no one really knows why there is this variation of colours).

12   13

Photos 12–13: Green and Brown forms of chrysalis (natural size 29mm).

In favourable years, when the July weather is particularly good, some of the pupae will change and give a summer brood of butterflies. This is a mathematically sound strategy as long as the weather remains good enough for the butterflies to breed and the autumn caterpillars to progress successfully. Either way, there are a large number of slumbering pupae, attached to the reeds, which hope to survive uneaten by predators until the following spring. In the old days, when fenmen cut the reeds for thatch, they would search for pupae, and store them safely until the following spring. A number were inevitably missed, and if thatching took place very quickly, this might explain the sightings of swallowtail butterflies in unlikely parts of the country. During the long period from July to the following May, many pupae would get eaten or perish. The following spring perhaps four new butterflies will emerge from each set of eggs, and this will allow the population to remain roughly stable. Our insect has passed though seven stages, five as a caterpillar, the sixth as a chrysalis, and the seventh as a butterfly.

In *As You Like It*, the laconic Jaques speaks of the seven ages of man.

> *All the world's a stage,*
> *And all the men and women merely players:*
> *They have their exits and their entrances;*
> *And one man in his time plays many parts,*
> *His acts being seven ages. At first, the infant,*
> *Mewling and puking in the nurse's arms...*
> *....Last scene of all,*
> *That ends this strange eventful history,*
> *Is second childishness, and mere oblivion,*
> *Sans teeth, sans eyes, sans taste, sans everything.*
> (*As You Like It*, Act 2, scene 7)

Shakespeare's man passes from infancy, through reluctant schooldays, to romantic love, brave soldiering, prosperity as a judge, before experiencing a gentle decline, which sets in with spectacles and slippers, and then becomes a sad second childhood with death as the unpalatable conclusion.

Our gallant Frenchman in the Impressionist gallery with his gracious view of Katharine in infancy, and the Swallowtail Butterfly both challenge the implicit futility of Shakespeare's seven ages. Instead of seven ages of man rising from a miserable infancy to the prime of life, and then descending to the helpless hopelessness of old age, we should see man as a spiritual being who, having passed through various natural stages, is suddenly challenged by God, and then perhaps, decisively, changed.

When Nicodemus came to see Jesus, he came by night to seek out and flatter a new teacher. He was astonished by Jesus' challenge 'I tell you the truth, no-one can see the kingdom of God unless he is born again' (John 3:3). Nicodemus was both puzzled and embarrassed by these words. He was not alone in this; throughout the next two thousand years these words have either been misunderstood or ignored. Nicodemus tried to bluff his way through with a rather feeble joke about the impossibility of re-entering his mother's womb. Jesus ignored this diversion and reinforced his words with an even more powerful statement, 'I tell you the truth, no-one can enter the kingdom of God unless he is born of water and the Spirit.' The good, cultured and well-educated Nicodemus received these strange words. His subsequent actions, first defending Jesus (John 7:50), and then helping Joseph of Arimathea to bury Jesus (John 19:39), showed how deeply the night-time encounter had affected him.

Nicodemus was a classic spiritual caterpillar. Caterpillars have only two aims: self-preservation and a good diet! Their life goes through many different stages. The Swallowtail caterpillar changes from being a tiny defenceless creature which imitates a bird dropping to become a beautiful and sophisticated one which has a reasonable prospect of escaping destruction. Nicodemus had advanced through the stages of his life, but had reached his spiritual limit. Until he met Jesus, there was little future. It was all going to be downhill thereafter, like the sixth and seventh ages of Jaques in *As You Like It*. We are all, by nature, spiritual caterpillars, selfish both about our well being (food) and our life (protection and camouflage).

Jesus pointed out to Nicodemus his need of rebirth through water and the Spirit. Water refers to the outward sign of baptism, and the Spirit to the inward gift that God offers to all who believe. Baptism is a sign of death to our old life, and union through the cross with the risen Christ. St Paul writes: 'Having been buried with him in baptism and raised with him through your faith in the power of God, who raised him from the dead' (Colossians 2:12).

Photo 14: Chrysalis showing wing colours of the future butterfly (natural size 29mm).

The caterpillar, in order to progress, has to go through a form of death. At first, many butterfly chrysalises look remarkably dead. Gradually, they show signs of life as the colours of the future butterfly appear in the miniature wings. The Swallowtail pupa can even survive under water in winter (thereby undergoing its own baptism?).

The emergence of the butterfly, as it bursts out of its winter tomb to new life, should be seen as a parable about spiritual rebirth. The transformation from caterpillar to butterfly is one of the wonders of our natural world. Although the caterpillar has embryonic wings, it certainly cannot fly! There is a nice cartoon of two caterpillars observing a passing butterfly. One says to the other: 'You certainly won't get me up in one of those things!' Unfortunately many people regard the possibility of spiritual rebirth with similar alarm. Frightened by the apparent excesses of some new Christians, unaware that the emergence is often part of a long spiritual process, they can all too easily remain as spiritual caterpillars. Scripture tells that, at this stage, the new disciple is like a newborn baby in need of spiritual milk so that he, or she, may grow up to salvation (see 1 Peter 2:2). The newly emerged butterfly is similarly helpless! Having broken out of the chrysalis case, it crawls to a 'safe' place, hangs upside down, and pumps lifeblood through its veins into its miniature wings. After a few minutes, they expand, and reach their full size. After this, the butterfly has to stay motionless (for several hours for our Swallowtail) until its wings are hard enough for flight. Then, at last, it is ready to fly away, feed, and search for a partner.

Photo 15: Underside of newly emerged butterfly just prior to first flight (natural size of hind-wing 38mm). Photo x1.7

It is a great privilege to observe the Holy Spirit at work in people long before they profess conversion. It is truly wonderful to see people being drawn as it were by a spiritual magnet, long before they are aware of what God is doing in their lives! St Mark records Jesus' opening message as proclaiming: 'The time has come, the kingdom of God is near. Repent and believe the good news!' (Mark 1:15). Repentance means turning away from self, dying to the old life, and preparing for a new one. People find this idea difficult. A former prime-minister, Mrs Thatcher, in a famous speech, declared that 'The Lady's not for turning' – good politics; but hopeless theology!

The newly emerged butterfly, provided it survives the precarious time of drying out its wings, has a new and wonderful freedom: freedom to fly, in some cases for thousands of

Photos 16: Close-up of wing patterns of newly emerged butterfly just prior to flight.
Photo x3

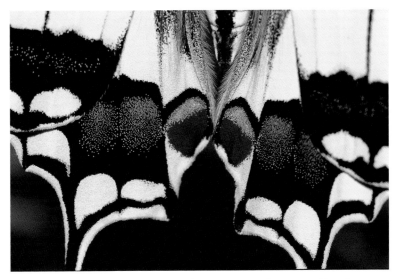

miles, freedom to taste a wide variety of nectar, freedom to fulfil its great biological aim to help to propagate the species!

The transformation of the newborn Christian should be far more wonderful. It is one of our greatest privileges to see this happening, sometimes before our own eyes.

Photo 17: Newly emerged British Swallowtail (note the slight but significant contrast with the lighter colouring, and narrower black veins, of the French Swallowtail at the beginning of the chapter – wingspan 75mm).
Photo natural size

As Christians, we must defy the pessimism of the laconic Jaques, and do more than Lear who laughed at gilded butterflies; our prayer, and effort, must be directed towards helping many more caterpillars to be transformed, by God's grace, into the glorious freedom, and fulfilment, that spiritual butterflies can and should experience!

CHAPTER
2

A Day in the Life of a Butterfly
(Growing up to Salvation)

"Pray for us now and at the hour of our birth."
(From 'Animula', T.S. Eliot)

The pages of Scripture give many delightful lessons from nature. The writer of Proverbs tells his readers to look to the ant and learn vital lessons about sloth, Peter (1 Peter 5:8–9) sees the Devil as a roaring lion, and Jesus (Matthew 6:26–27) uses God's care for the birds of the air to teach us about divine providence (well illustrated by one of our children's favourite books *The very worried sparrow*). Thus it seems reasonable to look to the newborn butterfly to teach us some important spiritual lessons.

The first minutes in the life of an adult butterfly are extremely hazardous. For several days, the colours of the miniature wings have been showing through the chrysalis, the pupa has been darkening and great cracks have been appearing. Suddenly, when the insect feels sufficiently powerful, it breaks the case of the pupa, and crawls out into a dangerous world. Usually, the newly emerged butterfly will hang upside-down, with its feet on the empty chrysalis case and its tiny embryonic wings hanging limply below its body. Hopefully, none of the chrysalis case will be attached to the wings – otherwise it will prove impossible to fully expand its

Photos 1–4: show how a chrysalis (natural size 21mm) changes before and during emergence. The word chrysalis is derived from Latin and literally means gold flecked. This is clearly illustrated here by the White Admiral pupa. The gold flecks give the chrysalis some protection from birds as they enhance the leaf like appearance of the chrysalis and look like sunlit raindrops. Photos x1.3

1

2

3

wings. Immediately, the butterfly starts to pump its body fluid along its wing veins. Like miniature balloons (and similar to the work of intricate by-pass heart surgery), the wings expand – growing visibly. This is an awesome sight which never fails to inspire an enraptured onlooker. Occasionally, the process is impeded. Fragments of the chrysalis case can remain attached to the butterfly, in which case the wings fail to expand properly (see photo below of the Comma). Sometimes the butterfly loses its grip, either through weakness or interference, and falls from its perch. In the wild, the unwanted arrival (for a female) of a predatory male, can lead to her wings never being properly expanded. Hopefully this will not occur. Having emerged, and expanded its wings, the butterfly needs time for them to dry and to harden. For some butterflies this seems to take an inordinately long time. In captivity, I have known Purple Emperors being unable to fly for a whole day.

The White Admiral, whose emergence I had awaited for much of a precious day-off, was ready to fly after about an hour. The newly emerged insect is completely defenceless. I have no idea what the mortality rate must be at this stage. Some fortunate butterflies (see chapter 9) are protected by friendly ants at this vulnerable time; most must take their chance in an unfriendly world.

The process of the new birth (see especially John 3:3–8 and 1 Peter 1:3, 23) is deeply mysterious. Sometimes the experienced evangelist can see the Holy Spirit working in someone's life long before they make any profession of faith. There is often a dissatisfaction and partial withdrawal from the things of the world; which is similar to the caterpillar's withdrawal and seeking a secluded place to pupate.

Then people often start to ask key spiritual and intellectual questions. This is frequently followed by an unexpected interest in prayer, the Bible and even in church and worship. There is a deep stirring within, as they realise that there must be more to life than they have so far discovered. This is similar to the advanced stage of the development of a chrysalis. When the wing colours start to show through the darkening pupa case (compare the first two photographs at the beginning of the chapter), you know that the butterfly is about to emerge!

Many times, I have seen this mysterious and wonderful process taking place as the human soul starts to be engaged by the Holy Spirit in the vital work known as regeneration. Helpers need to be very gentle at this stage. Too much interference can spoil the process which is in the main a transaction between God and a human being. Occasionally, the person, who shows a serious interest in the question of salvation, may need some encouragement to profess commitment, especially if he or she is dithering for too long. For the most part, the spiritual midwife should stand back and then look on with awe and wonder as the great emergence of the new-born Christian takes place.

Many new Christians would have a much better birth if all traces of their spiritual chrysalis case were removed. This particularly applies to past occult practice, which can cause great trouble in the future if not clearly renounced at the time of conversion.

Unlike the butterfly, which has no chance of satisfactory flight if it hasn't fully disentangled from the chrysalis, *the new disciple is given a life-time of opportunities to sort out the past*. But the more that is sorted out, released and repented of at the beginning, the more fruitful the disciple is likely to become.

After surviving the ordeal of emergence, the next task for

Photo 5: A Comma (wingspan 48mm) which had just emerged from a chrysalis in our garden has not been able to fully expand the wings closest to the camera. Photo x1.5

the newly-emerged butterfly is to feed. Butterflies feed in four main ways: by imbibing honey-dew, a sweet substance secreted by aphids which coats the leaves of many broad-leaved trees in summer; by feeding from the nectar of flowers; by 'mud-puddling' (a habit indulged in particularly by tropical species); and by licking salts from rocks and stony paths. They will also indulge (not always to their advantage) by feeding off the sap of damaged trees, and by gorging themselves on over-ripe fruit in an orchard or on a forest floor. Some species also have a penchant for animal dung or decayed carcasses. I am told that serious butterfly students never travel in Africa without a decaying rat – not perhaps the most endearing habit for fellow travellers! Recently I toured around France with a compote of over-ripe figs – thereby attracting some complaints, rather too many hornets, and a few spectacular butterflies!

The White Admiral feeds both from flowers and honeydew. It spends much of its life (which can last about a month) basking high up in oak trees, imbibing honeydew. The butterfly is most easily seen when it descends to feed from flowers (bramble blossom is a clear favourite), or when feeding off the dissolved salts of dung, or drinking water from a puddle on a sunny woodland path. Occasionally, they can be seen in a lovely courtship flight, soaring high into the sky in an exotic ritual dance.

In Europe, the Scarce Swallowtail is one of the easiest

Photo 6: The White Admiral (hind-wing 32mm) preparing to feed (note the proboscis half unfurled) from honeydew in Bernwood Forest. Photo x1.5

Photo 7: The Scarce Swallowtail (wingspan 80mm) resting briefly while feeding off Buddleia in southern France. Photo x1.2

butterflies to see, but one of the hardest to approach. One afternoon I saw one feeding on a buddleia bush beside a busy minor road in southern France. The wing colours were so bright, and the feeding so intense, that it was obviously newly emerged. The butterfly spent at least an hour, impervious to much photography, enjoying the nectar from the purple flowers. Like many butterflies when feeding, it kept on the move, walking round the flower-heads, with its long proboscis thrust deep allowing it to suck in the nectar with an action rather like a vacuum cleaner!

Photo 8: Tree Grayling (hind-wing 22mm) one of a huge colony which were all resting camouflaged and protected from the heat of the day in a wood in former Jugoslavia. Photo x1.5

Time spent in this way is essential if the butterfly is to survive. For some species, it may be just a matter of stocking up in case bad weather lies ahead, for others it is a matter of building up supplies to overcome either the perils of hibernation, or even the excessive heat of the summer. A Peacock butterfly emerging in July will need to absorb as much nectar as possible, so that it can enter the dangerous long months of hibernation well fed.

Some butterflies avoid intense heat, and rest for much

A field in Croatia full of flowers. Many butterflies will feast in such fields. Inset in the photo are (a) the Purple-Edged Copper (wingspan 34mm), (b) the Scarce Copper (wingspan 34mm), (c) the Mazarine Blue (wingspan 32mm) which was always rare in England and became extinct in the late 19th century. No one knows quite why, (d) the Glanville Fritillary (wingspan 40mm) is common in Europe, but in England is confined to the Isle of Wight. It is named after Lady Glanville whose relatives tried to contest her will on the grounds that only lunatics would pursue butterflies and (e) the Clouded Apollo (wingspan 60mm). The Apollo, a female, is wearing a sort of chastity belt implanted by a male to protect the purity of his seed. Interestingly this is called a sphragis, which is the Greek word that St Paul uses to describe the sealing of a believer by the Holy Spirit in 2 Corinthians 1:22, Ephesians 1:13 and 4:30.

of the day in deep shade. Tree Graylings spend much of their time sitting camouflaged on the bark of a tree, deep within pine forests, only occasionally emerging to take food or drink. Some species, such as the Meadow Brown in Italy, actually aestivate – that is, the butterfly spends several months, soon after emergence, resting. They will not reappear, from whatever cave or shady hollow they have used, until the cooler autumn weather comes. Then they will expect to mate and lay their eggs on growing, rather than withered, food-plants.

Mud-puddling is a butterfly feeding phenomenon well known in the tropics, and to a lesser extent in Europe. In favoured places, it is possible to see huge numbers of butterflies gathering near streams to drink and to feed. The most astonishing feeding that I have witnessed was in the Impenetrable Forest, near Bwindi, in south-west Uganda. After a long rough drive from one part of the forest towards the main nature reserve, we crossed a river. A few very large

Photo 9: Papilio
Hesperus (hind-wing
65mm), and numerous
Whites mud-puddling
by a river in Bwindi
National Park in south-
west Uganda.
Photo x0.7

swallowtails were flying. Not wishing to miss an opportunity,
I asked the driver to stop (the competent naturalist has a sort
of second sight when travelling!), and we got out. When I
clambered down to the wet sand under the bridge, I was met
by a truly astonishing sight. Thousands of butterflies of many
different species were gathered, jostling for places. One very
large Swallowtail was even clambering over the smaller
butterflies to get prime position! On this occasion, there
seemed to be a complete lack of predators.

At other times, I have watched small birds literally queuing
up alongside feeding butterflies waiting for their next meal. In
Europe, in midsummer, it is also common to see large
numbers of butterflies, and considerable varieties of species,
gathering where there is even a trace of moisture from which
they can feed.

Licking salts from stony paths seems to be the
characteristic behaviour of a number of male butterflies. It is
thought that males of many species need to absorb these salts

Photo 10 (Close-up): A Green Veined Charaxes (hind-wing 45mm) , in the Arusha National Park in Tanzania, so absorbed in the pleasures of feasting from animal dung that it could be approached to within a few inches. Photo x2

in order to become mature enough to mate successfully. Male Purple Emperors (see photos in chapter 11) often descend from their lofty oak trees for this purpose. This phenomenon is usually observed in the first week of their emergence, and takes place some time before the virgin females (which are primed to come out later) are on the scene. The large African Charaxes butterflies employ similar strategies, although their preference is for fresh animal dung. At such times, male butterflies become completely tame and can be picked up (they will then drink from the sweat of your finger) or photographed at incredibly close quarters.

For the new Christian, learning to feed from the Bible is essential. The word of God is vital food, and is often compared to honey – the favourite nectar of the butterfly! 'The ordinances of the Lord are sure and altogether righteous, they are more precious than gold, than much pure gold; they are sweeter than honey, than honey from the comb' (Psalm 19:9b–10).

'How sweet are your words to my taste, sweeter than honey to my mouth' (Psalm 119:103).

Without this vital food, the Christian will never grow, and will be vulnerable as soon as difficult times appear. There will be times when the Bible is a routine diet, helping the believer 'grow up to salvation'; there will be other times when the Bible speaks with incredible sweetness providing guidance, helping prayer ministry, clarifying deep-rooted problems, enlightening church matters, reminding about social concerns, etc. Christians who take trouble to study and memorise the Scriptures are greatly comforted and strengthened by them in times of illness and persecution. The persecutions of Brother Yun (note 1) were greatly alleviated by his encyclopaedic knowledge of Scripture.

We would be unwise to press the butterfly analogy too far, but it is observable that different butterflies have distinct preferences for certain flowers, and even colours of flower. For instance, it is known that mauve buddleia flowers are far more

Photo 11: The Dark Green Fritillary (hind-wing 29mm), in the Pyrenees, feeding from clover. The butterfly, which is very fast flying, is common in England and found in a much wider range of habitat than other British Fritillaries. Photo x2

attractive than other colours; and that butterflies with long tongues, such as Brimstones or Peacocks, enjoy the nectar of wild teasel and thistles; whereas butterflies like Gatekeepers which fly in the same sort of places, at the same sort of time, avoid these flowers because their tongues are too short.

The Song of Solomon has two interesting allusions to honey: 'Your lips drop sweetness as the honeycomb, my bride; milk and honey are under your tongue.' And 'I have come into my garden, my sister, my bride; I have gathered my myrrh with my spice. I have eaten my honeycomb and my honey; I have drunk my wine and my milk' (Song of Solomon 4:11 and 5:1). Many Christians (see chapter 4) interpret the song as an allegory of the relationship between Christ and his church (the bridegroom and the bride of Ephesians 5:22–33). Following this line of thought we can see the sweet nectar of honey (so valued in the ancient world and in places where sugar is unknown) as an allegory for the intimate relationship between Jesus and his people. This is expressed most clearly in the sacrament of Holy Communion. Different parts of Christendom may place greater emphasis on either word or sacrament: wise Christians will value both sources of spiritual honey.

Photo 12: A female Brimstone (hind-wing 30mm) feeding from thistles on the Ridgeway in Oxfordshire. The male, which is usually the first butterfly to be seen after hibernation, has bright yellow coloured wings from which the old name butter-coloured fly is thought to have been adapted to butterfly. Photo natural size

Not all food is helpful. Butterflies can become drunk, and then be unable to fly properly. Taking too much sap from a wounded tree, or drinking too much fermenting fruit juice from an orchard or forest floor can cause serious problems! It is fatally easy for Christians to get led into foolish ways – using 'sacred' texts which add or subtract from Scripture, or following dubious paths tinged with the subtle nectar of New Age spirituality with its dangerous emphasis on psychic experience, spiritualism, or even the worship of angels. Just as butterflies, such as the Red Admiral or the Camberwell Beauty, can fatally indulge in the orchard, or members of the Charaxes family can be easily attracted to overripe bananas or animal dung (see above), so it is possible for Christians to get distracted and move into byways which can do immense harm to their faith. The chapter in *The Pilgrim's Progress* which tells how Christian and Hopeful get trapped by Giant Despair within the grounds of Doubting Castle, is a celebrated literary example.

Feeding is a hazardous, but essential and pleasurable, task for the butterfly. But birds, dragonflies, spiders and lizards all wait as potential feasters upon feasting insects. The spider has a strategy which is simple. It either spins a web and waits, or it just rests hiding in, or near, a flower-head. The photograph (in chapter 10) of a Red Admiral preparing to feast on over-ripe blackberries shows a spider lurking, probably preparing for a pre-emptive strike. In the Alps, I approached an Apollo, displaying all its wing colours, apparently resting in a wild lavender bush. I then realised, as I have done on many subsequent occasions, that the butterfly was passively awaiting its fate, having been trapped in the delicate web of a subtle enemy. On this occasion I defied nature and freed the butterfly, which flew away with little apparent harm from its unwanted detention.

After food, the butterfly next requires shelter. Shelter is needed from cold and rain, from excessive heat, or just from the normal hazards of the night. Some butterflies roost very openly, others in groups under leaves.

Some years ago, in the Italian Alps, after two days of torrential rain, we discovered a deserted meadow full of

Photo 13: An Apollo Butterfly (wingspan 80mm) trapped in a spider's web at Allons in the foothills of the Alps in southern France. For many butterflies, lurking spiders play the part of the roaring lion in 1 Peter 5:8. Photo x0.5.
The Apollo was fortunate. In Argentina, we disturbed a Pansy butterfly. It flew into a spider's web. Immediately the predator descended on it and stung it fatally.

butterflies. That night, I was surprised to see many species, mainly blues and clouded yellows, openly sleeping high up on wisps of grass. The next day produced many sightings of other butterflies which had chosen to rest in less obvious ways (the lovely Purple-shot Copper, the strange and unusual snout-nosed Nettle-tree, and Cleodoxa, an unusual form of the High Brown Fritillary, spring to mind).

Peacock butterflies have an interesting defence mechanism. At night, and particularly during the long winter hibernation period, if disturbed they open their wings flashing their peacock 'eyes' (which some see as similar to small owls) and making a dramatic hissing sound. Even the sound of a single one (as I discovered in a coal shed in mid-winter) is quite startling! A whole platoon must scare off most predators without much difficulty.

Jesus told his disciples to 'come apart and rest awhile'. Wise Christians will have periods of withdrawal from the world, days or nights of prayer, and perhaps fasting. Far too many Christians suffer from burn-out. They would be wise to learn from the butterfly and take time to hibernate from the winter cold, or to aestivate from the heat of the summer.

Having survived the first night, the butterfly will

Photo14: The Small Blue (hind-wing 12mm), the smallest British butterfly, resting, with wings closed, quite openly. Many 'blue' butterflies sleep in very exposed places. Photo x3

instinctively open its wings. For many species, particularly some of the Swallowtails, Charaxes and Hairstreaks, this is the only time that they will be seen settled and with their wings open. It is essential for the butterfly to absorb the heat of the rays of the sun, so that its body temperature is raised enough to make flight possible. It is a wonderful sight to see a column of Soldier Commodores (a common African species), settled with military precision pointing their opened wings towards the morning sun. It is still more wonderful to see a normally fast flying swallowtail basking peacefully in the early sun. This is a photographer's dream! Most of the day these insects will

Photo 15: The Purple-shot Copper (wingspan 35mm) basking, and preparing to feed in the early morning in the Southern Alps. Photo x1.3

hurtle down tracks, briefly stopping as they visit flowers, usually walking around the flowers with wings fluttering, and when mud-puddling they will feed with their wings closed. The best time for photography is as the temperature begins to rise, a few minutes before the sun comes out (not always easy to predict!). The butterflies seem to anticipate this, and are very quiescent and approachable, opening their wings and waiting patiently for the sun's rays to do their work.

If the butterfly needs to spread its wings in the warmth of the sun, it is even more essential for the Christian to bask in prayer in the light of God's love and grace. Prayer has many parts including: confession, thanksgiving, praise, intercession, and adoration. The prayer of adoration occurs when someone

Photo 16: The Green Banded Swallowtail (wingspan 80mm) absorbing heat from the early morning sun in the Arusha National Park in Tanzania. The butterfly is resting deep in the long grass, where it has presumably just spent the night.
Photo natural size

at prayer relaxes silently in the warmth of God's love; meditating, like Isaac (Genesis 24:63) when awaiting the arrival of his bride. It is perhaps the most profound and most underused form of prayer. The Psalmist wrote so clearly, 'Be still, and know that I am God'; 'Find rest, O my soul, in God alone' (Psalms 46:10; 62:5); David knew the importance of what Isaiah later described as 'Quietness and Trust' (Isaiah 30:15). The prayer of adoration requires uncluttered, disciplined time. I have best experienced it in the silence of early morning prayers at the Franciscan house at Cerne

Photo 17: The White Admiral (wingspan 60mm) basking in the sun and preparing for its first flight.
Photo x1.1

Abbas. Half an hour of silence, sandwiched between Anglican Matins and breakfast made an inspirational start to a month of writing and prayer. From this quietness, we can learn to drink from the 'river of delights' and to experience what the Psalmist describes as 'the fountain of life' (Psalm 36:8–9). In our prayers we may sense the presence of God and feel spiritually on fire; with the result that the whole day, which lies ahead, is often transformed.

'Growing up to salvation' (1 Peter 2:2) is always a challenging process. Effective discipleship requires that the disciple knows how to feed on the word, how to rest, how to pray, how to be protected from the traditional enemies of the soul 'the world, the flesh, and the Devil'. The butterflies, in their dangerous journey, have plenty to show us!

Note
1. Brother Yun, *The Heavenly Man* (Monarch, 2002).

He has made everything beautiful

Ecclesiastes 3:11

Three Tailed Hairstreak in Bwindi, Uganda

CHAPTER 3

Migration and Mimicry
(Mission and the Imitation of Christ)

"I'll put a girdle round about the earth in forty minutes."
(Puck to Oberon: *A Midsummer Night's Dream*, Act 1, Scene 2)

The mystery of butterfly migration

In 1869, a man was riding near the Dead Sea when 'he noticed that the whole mass of grass, through which they were riding on camels, was in a state of violent agitation although there was no wind. When he dismounted he discovered that the cause was the emergence from the chrysalis of myriads of Painted Lady butterflies, which dried their wings and about half an hour later flew off together eastwards towards the sea' (note 1).

Nobody really knows what triggers these migrations; the Painted Lady is the world's most migratory butterfly; like Puck it has truly put a girdle round about the earth and can be found almost anywhere except in South America. In England, we benefit from a regular invasion of three beautiful migrants, some other familiar butterflies have their numbers supplemented by migration, and a few other very rare migrants appear from time to time.

Our three regular migrants, the Red Admiral, the Painted Lady and the Clouded Yellow, can be seen in enormously varied numbers every year. They brighten our summer, enrich our autumn, but none of them is truly a resident of our country.

The Red Admiral, doyen of many gardens, flies in from North Africa, Spain and others part of Europe. It can reach as far north as the Shetland Isles, and apparently is often seen in Lapland! Why it generally fails to survive our winters is a bit of a mystery. Recently, there is some evidence that with our warmer winters a few are managing to hibernate. In 1996, I saw some in Dorset in late March and I've seen them at similar times in Somerset and in Devon. But for the most part, our gardens are filled in late summer with the offspring

Photos 1–4: This sequence shows the caterpillar, larval tent, chrysalis and wing close-up of the Red Admiral (natural sizes 15mm, 15mm, 23mm, and hind-wing 35mm)

of summer migrants who have arrived and bred here. Breeding is pretty simple for the Red Admiral, unlike the Peacock and the Small Tortoiseshell – almost any nettle will do!

The caterpillar lives in a small tent and, although liable to attack by a parasitic wasp, a good number survive. By the late autumn, in a favourable year, many can be seen jostling with wasps to feed on the nectar of ivy flowers. Then, if the butterfly is wise, a reverse migration, south, will take place. Just once, many years ago, I saw this happening. I was walking down Kingsgate Street in Winchester, which runs North-South, and I was aware of dark butterflies flying above me. There must have been at least thirty at about twenty second intervals, flying due south on their way back to a warmer winter in Spain or North Africa.

The Painted Lady, one of the world's most widespread butterflies (I have seen them in Central Africa, where there English name causes considerable amusement, as well as throughout Europe), is a well-known migrant. Apparently someone recorded a migration in 1272! In April 1996 I was aware of many Painted Ladies in the south of France. I noticed one female searching with great care for a small new thistle on which to lay her eggs. She used her feet to choose the right plants, and would only lay an egg on very small plants which would have some chance of survival as the ground dried up. About a month later, in a low mountain pass, still in the south of France, I saw about 50 Painted Ladies resting on rocks; obviously waiting to move north.

Photo 5: Part of a large group of Painted Ladies resting on warm rocks prior to their migration north.

That year, by mid August, there were so many Painted Ladies in England that even the newspapers were commenting on the phenomenon. Two years later, the Painted Lady had such a bad year in England that I saw almost as many in a brief foray in Uganda as in the whole summer and autumn at home.

What seems to happen, although exactly how, why and when is unclear, is that the butterflies realise that their food-plants, mainly thistles, are drying up, and that to lay eggs on them is a waste of effort. By some deep instinct, they move north, and those that reach England encounter fewer enemies; thus it is possible for each generation to multiply by a considerable factor – perhaps as large as fifty. As each new generation can come through in about five weeks, in a hot summer numbers can build up dramatically. Like the Red Admiral, the Painted Lady has little hope of surviving our winter, and the butterflies must emigrate south or perish.

The Clouded Yellow is a distinctive migrant, its golden-yellow colouring making it clearly different from the male Brimstone.

Photo 6: A typical sighting of the Clouded Yellow (hind-wing 30mm) feeding off red clover, which is also its main breeding plant. Unfortunately, in this country, clover is often cut just after the migrant Clouded Yellows have laid their eggs. Photo x1.5

The Clouded Yellow has some years of great abundance. Some are seen almost every year in the Isle of Wight and on the coastlines of Devon and Cornwall. In a favourable year, it breeds successfully on clover, and the population moves steadily north. 1983 was a particularly good year. I remember releasing some butterflies in early October which had emerged from caterpillars that I had been given. As I released the first one, a wild one appeared in the same field.

The most remarkable English migrant, and indeed probably the most remarkable migrant on our planet, is the Monarch, or Milkweed. Occasionally these unmistakeable large orange butterflies arrive in the south-west of England. In 1981, perhaps a hundred were seen in Cornwall and the

Photo 7: The Bath White (hind-wing 24mm, a very rare migrant which acquired its name because a lady in Bath stitched a likeness of the butterfly on a pocket handkerchief!). Other rare migrants include Pale and Berger's Clouded Yellows, Long and Short-tailed Blues; the Queen of Spain Fritillary, the Camberwell Beauty and the Monarch. Some common resident butterflies such as the Large White, the Small White and the Small Tortoiseshell also migrate to this country. The Swallowtail (see chapter 1) also migrates from France to Kent in some years which included 2003. Photo x1.7

Scilly Islands. The Monarch is a native of Mexico, USA and Canada. Its extraordinary life cycle is now well known. For years, the fall in North America has been enlivened by clouds of Monarchs migrating southwards. Many head for a small area of mountains in Mexico. Here millions of Monarchs hibernate together; in the following spring the survivors wake up and then set off on a return flight of some thousand miles north towards the main breeding ground. This takes several generations, eggs are laid in the south, and emerging butterflies continue to fly north. It is probably the fourth generation which, with some amazing homing instinct, sets off south again the following autumn.

In about 1860, the Monarch achieved some dramatic migrations and established colonies not only in Australia, New Zealand and other Pacific Islands, but also in the Azores and the Canary Islands. From there Spain and Portugal have been colonised.

Butterflies as mimics and models

As well as being remarkable migrants, the Danaids (the Monarch family) are also crucial in the study of mimicry. Butterfly mimicry, long observed but still not fully understood, takes two main forms. The most interesting, called Batesian mimicry, occurs when species gain protection from predators such as birds by adopting the colouration, and to some extent the habits, of more numerous but poisonous butterflies. Most of the Danaids are highly toxic to birds and will have come from caterpillars which have fed on poisonous milkweed plants. One unpalatable meal should be sufficient to deter most birds from attempting to digest these insects! Obviously, if another butterfly is a sufficient look-alike it should gain protection from the same predators. The other form of mimicry, called Mullerian, occurs when similar species gain mutual protection because birds learn that a particular species is toxic, and then from the principle of safety in numbers, other similar species are protected.

The Common Tiger, an African relative of the Monarch which like the Monarch has colonised the Canary Islands and parts of Spain, is an excellent model for a number of species to mimic. The Diadem, a common African butterfly, is an excellent mimic, which manages to model all four distinctive forms of the Common Tiger. Interestingly, only the female Diadem has this protection. The male, a striking black butterfly with white spots edged with shot purple, is completely different and receives no protection. I remember spending a hot afternoon attempting to photograph African butterflies in the garden of the Sunset Hotel in Kisumu. Very few would settle (a common experience in the heat of the day), and I was glad to approach what I thought was the Common Tiger. It proved much more amenable than I expected, and allowed a few photographs. I then realised that it was the mimic, the Diadem, which perhaps because of its inbuilt protection felt safer than the model. By contrast, male Diadems which lack the protection of mimicry, are very difficult to approach, and almost impossible to photograph!

One of the most fascinating of all African butterflies is the

Photos 8–11: The Common Tiger, or African Queen (upper and underside, wingspan 80mm); and two mimics – the female Diadem (wingspan 80mm) and Pseudacraea Deludens (hind-wing 40mm).

Mocker Swallowtail, which is also known as the Flying Handkerchief. This large cream coloured butterfly is frequently seen in African gardens and forests. It gets its colloquial name, the Mocker, from the extraordinary variety and habits of its females. It is thought to have up to 200 forms ranging from tailed females in Madagascar and Ethiopia through to a bewildering mass of tailless, variously coloured forms throughout the rest of Africa which are each thought to mimic a different but locally common species.

Professor Sir Cyril Clarke, of Liverpool University, did a great deal of research on the Mocker Swallowtail. By cross breeding stock from different female forms, he made a lot of practical discoveries in the field of genetics, and was able to translate this into research about the cause and cure of rhesus blue babies. He also established that the different female forms

12

13

14

Photos 12–14: The Mocker Swallowtail (male), upper and underside (wingspan 100mm) and, probably, one of the many female forms (note the similarity of the body markings of the tailless female and the tailed male).

had gradually evolved in their different surroundings, slowly adapting according to outward circumstances.

The call to be missionaries

Butterflies migrate by instinct, and model other species for protection. Christians migrate by a mixture of spiritual intuition and command, and model Jesus (and to a much lesser extent other leaders) by grace and obedience. Christians were given their migration orders on the first Ascension Day when Jesus said:

'But you will receive power when the Holy Spirit comes on you; and you will be my witnesses in Jerusalem, and in all Judea and Samaria, and to the ends of the earth' (Acts 1:8).

It took a while for the first Christians to obey the message. Not until the persecution which resulted in the martyrdom of Stephen (Acts 8) did the church really move out from Jerusalem. The conversion of Paul and his subsequent three missionary journeys established the church in much of Greece and the Roman Province of Asia. Meanwhile, other missionaries brought the church to Rome. Despite huge waves of persecution, brave missionaries took the gospel to the corners of the known world. By the time of the conversion of the Emperor Constantine (in the fourth century), Christianity had spread far and wide.

Many centuries later, there was a new flowering of missionary activity, and the gospel was taken to South America, much of Africa, China, Australasia, India and other parts of Asia. In the last few years, there has been a further resurgence of mission, spreading out from Singapore and China. Many people, answering a deep inner call, have given their lives, or the best years of their life, to the mission field.

In this new millennium, many young people are giving time to serve the needs of the poor in the third world, and taking a gospel of social action, healing and salvation with them. It is difficult to say exactly how this all happens; but often deep within the human soul, especially when united with Christ, there is a desire to serve overseas. This migration, even if quite temporary, is always costly – taking its toll physically, emotionally and financially. Yet almost all who feel the call to serve in this way return home deeply moved and spiritually strengthened.

I will give just two examples. At the age of 60, my mother-in-law, Elizabeth Feilden, received an unlikely call to go and serve the rural poor in western Kenya. For some 17 years, she has lived much of the year in Kenya – first in tents, and then in permanent buildings. The call has involved her in much sacrifice (in health with regular bouts of malaria; in finance; and in struggles with local jealousies and financial corruption); but there have been many gains. The lives of many poor farming families have been transformed by learning how to use their land better, and in some cases by the precious gift of a cow; some people have learnt useful skills, many have been employed; evangelism has been undertaken particularly through the JAM (Jesus and Me) factory which has inspired many young people, and now has an independent life of its own. Some teaching about medical health, especially concerning HIV, has been brought, and many families now have improved and enriched diets. Elizabeth's dedication has inspired her grandchildren. All my own family have spent serious time in Africa as a result of her lead, which has also influenced their faith. Rachel, my eldest daughter, started the JAM factory on one of her summer visits. Susie has spent much time in Uganda and launched a woman's charity in Kabale; Tim has helped lead an effective mission in the area near Elizabeth's project; and Katy, our youngest, has spent part of a gap year teaching in Tanzania. My own call to be involved in short missions to Africa was made much clearer by seeing Elizabeth's inspiration and sacrifice.

The most inspirational book that I've read for many years is *The Heavenly Man* (see note at the end of chapter 2). This extraordinary story of evangelism, miracles and persecution within China has its roots in the old missionary movement which expired when the communists ejected all the western missionaries in 1949. Brother Yun's conversion resulted from the dramatic healing of his father from cancer – his mother offering prayer in the way that she could just remember from the missionaries about twenty-five years earlier. Yun quickly became a very effective evangelist leader in part of the underground church. He was frequently arrested, imprisoned and tortured. After a dramatic escape from a high security prison, Yun escaped to the West. But his inspiration now is the 'Back to Jerusalem' mission. This extraordinary vision, stemming from a group of believers of whom all but one died in prison, was passed on to Yun in 1995. It could well prove to be one of the most sacrificial, and effective, missions of all time as it seeks to reach Jerusalem through following ancient trade routes through Buddhist, Hindu and Muslim lands.

Most Christians understand the call to evangelise in their

own locality, but some have a deep call to fulfil the great commission (Matthew 28:18–20) and to take the gospel all over the world. No one can tell what stirs the Painted Lady to leave the sunny regions of Africa, and to head north on an uncertain journey; but each missionary who is truly called knows who is calling them and has some idea of what they have to do.

Photo 15: A Painted Lady (wingspan 65mm), newly emerged in England. Photo x1.5

The imitation of Christ

Christians are also called to be imitators of others. Paul puts it very clearly:

'Be imitators of me, as I am of Christ.'
(1 Corinthians 11:1, RSV)

'Therefore I urge you to imitate me.'
(1 Corinthians 4:16)

'Be imitators of God, therefore, as beloved children.'
(Ephesians 5:1, RSV)

Imitation of Christ is a classic theme of the New Testament, and of later Christian writing. It is quite different from butterfly mimicry! Butterflies mimic their models to try and avoid trouble; Christians try to imitate Christ, and in many countries and in many situations, the more they succeed the greater the trouble they can expect. Jesus constantly warned his followers to expect trouble. Indeed, they were to rejoice in it when it came! The areas in which we are particularly called to imitate Jesus include prayer, regular worship, honouring and using the word of God, sacrificial lifestyle, dependence on God in everyday living, servanthood, very high moral standards for ourselves and yet incredible generosity and forgiveness to those who fall short, a freedom of living that defies local culture and religious taboos, authority over the powers of darkness, peace, joy and self-giving love. Most of us will find this an uncomfortable list. We are happy to look to Jesus for forgiveness, protection, healing and new life – just as a butterfly mimic might gain from its association with its model. If we are honest, we are a good deal less comfortable when following Jesus involves risk, financial disadvantage, loss of status in the world, and the danger of losing both face and friends as we seek to share the good news! In 1526, William Tyndale completed his translation of the New Testament into English. It was to cost him his life, but his great work, smuggled into England from Antwerp, brought the means of salvation to many in England. Interestingly, Tyndale uses the word 'counterfeit' instead of 'imitate'. Counterfeit has changed its meaning in the course of the last 500 years. Today, the Diadem certainly counterfeits the Common Tiger and the better the counterfeit, the safer the butterfly; in many parts of the world, as Christians imitate Jesus the better the imitation, the more they run into peril!

Note

1. Jeremy Thomas, *The Butterflies of Britain and Ireland* (Dorling Kindersley, 1991), p. 119.

CHAPTER 4

Many Waters Cannot Quench Love
(Love)

"She was then the prettiest, silliest, most affected, husband-hunting butterfly she ever remembers."

This well-known comment (written in a letter in 1815 about the great author Jane Austen) displays a wonderful ignorance about the ways of butterflies; I rather hope it displays a similar innaccuracy about Jane Austen, whose writing so many of us read with so much pleasure.

In the matter of courtship and mating, male butterflies (usually smaller and more brightly coloured) normally take the initiative. In most species, the males emerge first and spend awhile maturing. Males of many species (see photographs in chapter 2) can be seen mud-puddling, feeding off animal dung or from damp patches on stony pathways. They are thought to be absorbing vital salts, which are thought to be necessary for their full sexual development.

Male butterflies appear to have a number of mating strategies. One afternoon I was taken to visit a windmill, le Moulin de Bagor, which stands high above the little village of Valprionde, in the Valley of the Lot. The windmill had been magnificently, and lovingly, restored by its proud owner. After a detailed inspection, we descended. I casually surveyed the large field of ripe wheat that lay below the windmill – hardly expecting it to be a paradise for butterflies. It was mid July, and the two common French Swallowtails, the bright yellow one (le grand porte-queue; photo chapter 1), and the elegant cream one with black stripes (le flambe; photo chapter 2) were both flying in the locality. I was suddenly aware that the field was alive with both species. In quite a small segment of the field, I could see at least fifty butterflies. The windmill was situated at the highest point in the surrounding countryside, and the Swallowtails were adopting a variant of the African strategy of hill-topping. The French males had found a simple strategy: they waited perched on the tallest wisps of wheat, and judging by the number of aerial courtship displays taking place above the field, the females were obliging by turning up in large numbers!

True hill-topping is a spectacular phenomenon. One of my favourite places in Africa is Kakamega rain forest in western Kenya (see chapter 8). This jewel of natural history is home to many birds, butterflies, snakes, wonderful trees and many other natural marvels. The forest, and its surrounds, contains many butterfly species – some with huge populations. Many are found flying down the few sunlit tracks; others can be seen high up in the forest canopy feeding off honey-dew on the leaves. I was surprised to be taken to walk up to the top of a small bare grassy hill, which dominates one

Photo 1: A pair of Giant Charaxes (wingspan 110mm) preparing to mate, after meeting when hill-topping above Karkamega Forest, which can be seen in the background. Photo x0.5

part of the forest. It took quite a while to climb. We walked through long grass, keeping a wary look-out for snakes. After about half-an-hour's walk, we reached the summit. This was a flat rectangular area, about 50 metres long and rather less wide, from which we obtained a spectacular view of the forest, approaching thunderstorms, and butterflies! Many large butterflies, including the Giant Charaxes, were using this area as a meeting place. I was amazed to see the Charaxes flying with such speed and determination that they could drive birds away! A few minutes later, I saw a pair of Kenya's largest butterflies, the Regal Swallowtail, flying very slowly around the hill-top. A slow leisurely courtship was beginning.

2

Photo 2: The Regal Swallowtail, Kenya's largest butterfly (wingspan 130mm or more), and the Beautiful Tiger (wingspan 100mm) which as a member of the Monarch family is poisonous to birds. The Regal Swallowtail is thought to mimic it, although their very different sizes make this seem far from certain. The colours of the Swallowtail have faded considerably due to longevity.
Photos x2/3

Later they would soar into the sky, pirouette and chase one another, before descending to the forest canopy to complete what their hill-top tryst had begun.

Many species meet in other ways. Some live in large colonies. The Adonis Blue is a good example. On a favourable hillside, where their foodplant (horseshoe vetch) grows, they can be found in large numbers. A strong healthy male is likely to have little difficulty in finding a suitably willing partner. Sheer numbers, and the confined space of the colony, make the task simple. By contrast, the Silver-spotted Skipper, which is confined in England to about 50 areas of warm downland in the south and east of England, lives in small colonies. Females are often detected by the scent which they emit; a hopeful male will then allow his sex-brand to burst open and to shower scent scales over his intended partner (see photo of Silver-spotted Skippers courting – the male's sex-brand is clearly visible). After a tumbling aerial courtship, they usually settle with the male sitting just behind the female, preparing to mate.

Some males, of many different species, adopt a territorial approach. They find a perch or a pathway, and patrol this restlessly, hoping that a female will pass by. The Small Copper is very territorial, and will rise fom his station to drive away invaders, including insects much larger than himself.

Walking along a pathway, I disturbed a male Peacock butterfly. He had survived the winter, and was now in pursuit of a partner. He followed me and circled around me for about 100 metres, thereby making it abundantly clear that I was on his territory and most unwelcome. I also remember walking

Photo 3: A pair of Silver-spotted Skippers (wingspan 30mm, hind-wing 15mm) preparing to mate. Note the male's dark sex-brand on his forewings. According to Professor Ford, while female butterfly scent is undiscernible to us, the scent of male butterflies is often strong and attractive. For instance, the Green-veined White gives off a strong scent of Lemon Verbena! Photo x2

along a forest pathway in the Bwindi Impenetrable Forest in Uganda. Male Charaxes butterflies were racing up and down the narrow track. One particular blue male, very large and double-tailed as most of the Charaxes are, passed us several times. I was wearing a bright blue shirt. After a while, it took great exception to my presence, circled around me, landed on me, and even seemed to be trying to attack me with the sharp tails at the edge of its wings! It clearly saw me, or my bright blue shirt, as undesirable competition in its chosen territory.

Another strategy is to use what the old entomologists call a master tree. This tree, usually very prominent, is a place where the males gather and wait for females to appear in the locality. This tactic is adopted by some species, especially those with a low population density. For instance, often there will be only a small number of Brown Hairstreaks which emerge from a large area of sloe. The males make for a suitable ashtree, and by some instinct, or perhaps scent, the females know where to look for a partner. Such trees are hard to find, and are often closely guarded secrets. Just twice, I have seen such a tree. In Wiltshire, near Sailsbury, when Purple Emperors were much more abundant in the 1970s, there was a fine tall

Photo 4: Small Copper (wingspan 35mm) perched on a typical territorial post. Photo x2

oak tree on the edge of a minor road. It stood at the entrance of a nature reserve, which had plenty of sallow – the breeding plant for the females. On a good afternoon in July, it was possible to see a number of male Purple Emperors sunning themselves on the higher branches (see chapter 11 for photographs). Sometimes they would take off to drive away other species such as Silver-washed Fritillaries and White Admirals; at other times they would attempt to see off another Emperor who had come too close to their perch. Great flashes of purple could be seen as the males did battle in the airspace around the tree. Victorian entymologists tell of capturing successive males on the same branch of such a tree (although how they managed it judging by the height of the Wiltshire tree is quite beyond me). Eventually, the leading male will be rewarded by the approach of a passing female. Then they head off for higher ground and elaborate courtship. I once witnessed this at the top of a small hill in the foothills of the Pyrenees.

Once when watching Europe's largest butterfly, the Two-tailed Pasha (*Charaxes Jasius*, the only Charaxes in Europe – there are 179 species in Africa), I stumbled upon a master tree. The Two-tailed Pasha breeds on the strawberry tree, which is a common scrub plant for about 50 miles inland from the Mediterranean coast. It was a very hot day in July; I was aware of the butterflies, resplendent with deep chocolate brown upper wings, edged with gold and two long tails, hurtling past me. Occasionally the butterflies settled on a leaf, or on the pebbled beach of a dried-up stream. Their mottled underside was beautifully camouflaged, and the butterfly almost unapproachable to photograph. The weather was incredibly hot. Eventually, in desperation hoping to see them better, I waited under a small scrubby tree (but perhaps the largest that was around) and laid out a bait of over-ripe banana, spiced with a little red wine. From nowhere butterflies queued up to imbibe. For one glorious moment, I was aware of six feeding from my banana, and another three pairs engaged in courtship flight. The little scrub tree seemed to be both their meeting and their resting place. (See insert on pages 58–59 for a full sequence of this butterfly's life-cycle.)

Silver-washed fritillaries have a splendid courtship flight and then land close together, with antennae touching, while the male sits quivering with his wings half open. These beautiful butterflies can still be found, often in very large numbers, in open woodland in the south and south-west of England.

Most butterflies pair discreetly, often under leaves, or high up in the canopy. If disturbed, they take off in a somewhat clumsy flight, the larger female flying while the smaller male rests his wings. They soon land, and seek another period of solitude. The union can last at least an hour. When it is over, the male leaves to feed and look for further conquests; the female, while her eggbatch ripens, tries to hide from other males and predators. Then she sets about her business of egg laying which, in some species, may carry on until her last day.

The Scriptures have a great deal to teach us about the relationship between the sexes. There are many sad stories of predatory males, and beguiling females. There are many

Photos 5–8: pair of romantic Silver-washed Fritillaries (wingspan male 65mm, female 70mm) with antennae touching, a male and two female butterflies, including the unusual valezina form of the female. Valezina females have an inherited gene which produces the beautiful silvery-grey colouration. They can account for up to 15% of some populations, but are completely absent from others. They seemed very common on the banks of the Endre in southern France, and I have often seen them in Wiltshire.

Photo 9: A pair of Orange Sprites (wingspan 32mm), members of the skipper family in the Arusha National Park, Tanzania. Photo x2

warnings against the misuse of sex; but there are also some very beautiful stories. There is one book, the Song of Songs, whose main theme is about the wonder, and passion, of young love. It would be easy to move from the world of rapacious male butterflies, and a few hungry husband-hunting females, into the disaster stories of Old and New Testament. But bearing in mind the elegance of many butterflies in courtship; it would seem better to look at a happier theme.

Courtship in Britain seems to belong to a by-gone age: an age in which a young man and a young woman would declare an interest in each other, and spend time getting to know each other – their interests, their hopes, their spirituality and even their failings. The process might be quite brief, as with Boaz and Ruth (Ruth 2–4); or take many years, as with Jacob and Rachel (Genesis 29). Consummation of young love was delayed, in Christian and many other circles, until the wedding night. The engagement time (bethrothal in the Old Testament was even more formal) was spent romantically, enjoying each other's company, making plans, and getting to know each other's family. There were, despite obvious temptations, clear sexual boundaries. Marriage 'is an honourable estate, instituted of God himself, signifying unto us the mystical union that is betwixt Christ and his Church' (*Book of Common Prayer* 1928, Preface to the Marriage Service). Marriage was, and is, God's plan for all those that he doesn't call into the more difficult state of celibacy (see Matthew 19:11–12). The poetic account of romantic love in the Song of Songs encourages us to realise how highly Scripture values a proper use of sex. The fact that both Catholics and Puritans, from very different theological persuasions, have seen the Song as an allegory of the relationship between Christ and his church (see also Ephesians 5:22–33) in no way invalidates this. One passage from the Song reminds an entomologist of the romantic pursuits of the butterfly:

Come my lover, let us go to the countryside, let us spend the
*   night in the henna bushes.*
Let us go early to the vineyards to see if the vines have budded,
If their blossoms have opened, and if the pomegranates are in
*   bloom —*
There I will give you my love.

(Song of Songs 7:11–12)

Photo 10: A pair of Silver-studded Blues (wingspan 30mm) courting. The female, typically of many of the Blue species, has the sombre dark colouring. Photo x1.3

If we could recapture the restrained, but highly romantic, courtship of the past, many more marriages would begin with pure excitement rather than with a piece of legal paper and a sense of deja-vu from a couple who have already lived under the same roof, and usually slept in the same bed, for many years. A few lessons from the elegant free flight of courting butterflies would not come amiss!

It is generally agreed that most female butterflies only mate once. They will then attempt to lay between 100 and 500 eggs; some species lay in great clusters, others singly. The species which hibernate, like the Peacock, and the Large Tortoiseshell, seem to lay a particularly large number of eggs. Probably they need to start the winter with a large number of butterflies per eggbatch. Hibernation will inevitably decimate the numbers, and there must be enough survivors to breed again in the following spring.

Watching a female laying her eggs is fascinating. In all species, it is noticable that the female butterfly flies in a much slower purposeful way. She flies around plants, then landing, testing the plant with her feet. This way she can 'taste' that she has landed on a suitable plant; then she will curve her abdomen and deposit a single egg on the leaf. In Bentley Wood, in Wiltshire, where White Admirals are plentiful, I watched a female fluttering over some bramble and bushes which were tangled together. A small wisp of her foodplant,

Photo 11: The underside of a female Silver-studded Blue, showing the silver discs which give it the name (hindwing 15mm). Photo x1.5

honeysuckle, was present. Unerringly, she discovered it, and laid her egg in full sunshine. This was unusual, as for the most part, White Admirals seek out honeysuckle in the shadier parts of the wood, in order to lay their eggs. In southern France, I watched the Southern White Admiral doing the same work. She chose a plant already inhabited by a tiny caterpillar. The White Admiral caterpillar, when tiny, eats its food plant in such a distinctive way that it is quite easy to find. (See photo in chapter 6.)

Photo 12: A small bush full of Silver-studded Blues gathering for food, and perhaps for courtship.

Butterflies such as the Small Tortoiseshell, which lay their eggs in large batches, choose the underside of leaves where they are less conspicuous. I watched the Spotted Fritillary, a common butterfly in southern Europe, start to lay an egg batch, until I carelessly disturbed her when attempting some photography. Some of the larger butterflies seem to dive at trees and bushes, and lay an egg within a split second. I have seen Purple Emperors doing this high up in sallow bushes; and Scarce Swallowtails attacking sloe with a delicate circular approach, choosing the right plant with great accuracy.

By contrast some members of the Brown family, whose foodplants will be various grasses, lay their eggs (so I am told) with abandon — sometimes even when in flight. The Scotch Argus lays her eggs deep in the tussocks of purple moor grass — even experts find her eggs almost impossible to find.

Photo 13: The Spotted Fritillary (hind-wing 20mm) laying some of her eggs in southern France. Photo x2

Some females can live a long time beyond their egg-laying period (Brimstones and Camberwell Beauties seem to survive way beyond this time — both butterflies lay their eggs in the spring but can be seen flying in high summer); others are still laying when their wings are tattered and torn, determined even when old and weak to deposit as much of their precious cargo as possible.

There seems to be one more thing that we could learn from this part of the butterfly life-cycle. As well as the importance of the courtship, we should also marvel at the single-minded determination of the female butterfly to preserve her species. After the resurrection, Jesus gave his disciples one simple command: 'Go out and make disciples' (Matthew 28:19). If we displayed as much dilgence in obeying this command as female butterflies do the laying of their eggs, the gospel would be flourishing much more strongly in Britain, and Western Europe.

The author, photographed by his wife, photographing butterfly eggs in the south of France (see overleaf).

The Two-tailed Pasha is the only European member of the Charaxes family which has nearly 200 members in Africa. The butterfly is found in Mediterranean coastal districts, its larval foodplant is the wild strawberry tree. Butterflies fly in May/June and have a second generation in August/September. The photographic sequence shows the very striking eggs on the foodplant, the escape of the tiny caterpillar, caterpillar stage through to the dramatic pupation sequence where the pupa has to perform a 'long jump' when having escaped from the larval skin it has to use its cremasters to get hooked onto the prepared pad of silk. Then we see the chrysalis darkening, the colours of the wings showing through, and the emergence of the adult butterfly. This sequence was photographed between mid July and mid September. The butterfly is quite common wherever its foodplant grows, and is attracted by ripe figs and other fruit. Natural sizes: eggs height 1.00mm; small caterpillars from 1mm to fully grown at 60mm; chrysallis 35mm; butterfly wingspan 82mm.

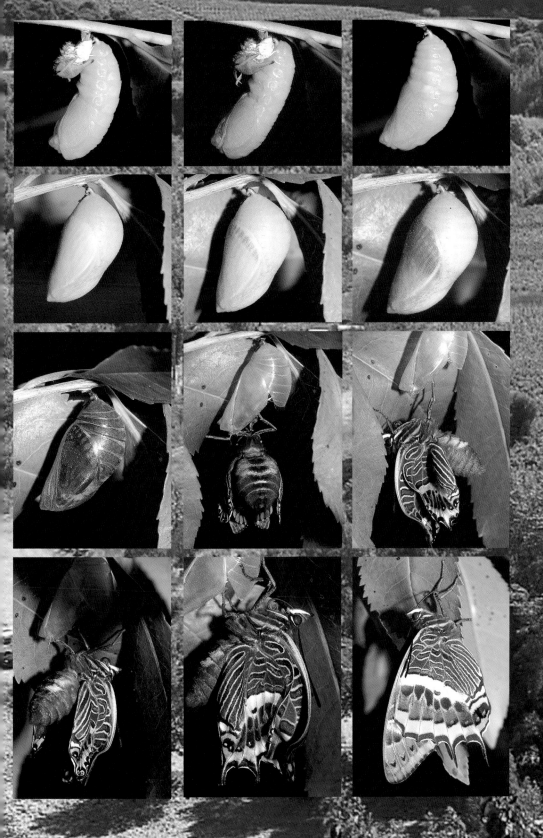

CHAPTER

5

Of Hairstreaks and a Forbidden Marsh

(Sin)

"I only ask to be free. The butterflies are free. Mankind will surely not deny to Harold Skimpole what it concedes to the butterflies."

(Charles Dickens, *Bleak House*, chapter 6)

The Hairstreaks are one of my favourite families of butterfly. All are elusive and each initial encounter gave me a theological insight. I met the Green Hairstreak on a natural history expedition, in 1970, from Winchester College to the New Forest. It fell to me, as a chauffeur who had escaped from umpiring cricket, on what was billed as an 'adder hunt', to make the most significant find. A small green butterfly was disturbed from a gorse bush. There was a cry of 'catch it', and a beautiful tiny electric-green coloured butterfly landed in my borrowed net. A new world opened up. A childhood love of butterflies was rekindled at a time when my life was in considerable disarray (including amongst other things, the tragic death of both my parents in the previous year and an uncertain start at the wrong theological college). The Green Hairstreak gave me a new interest and fresh hope. Soon afterwards, on the floor of some oak woodland in Wiltshire, I saw a small purple jewel glistening amidst the moss. A newly-emerged Purple Hairstreak was flashing its iridescent wings as it prepared for its first flight. The brilliance of this tiny butterfly did much to compensate for the elusive aloofness of the Purple Emperors disporting themselves in the canopy above.

Five years later, Jane and I were walking in the Cothill Marshes. Our first child, Rachel, was due and Jane wanted a walk to hurry nature along. We passed a familiar stile. Memories of 'breaking bounds' from Cothill School to make water courses in the marshes flooded back. This

Photo 1: A Green Hairstreak (Hind-wing 15mm). Green Hairstreaks, when settled, are very well camouflaged. Their upper wings are very dark; consequently they are also inconspicuous when flying. Photo x1.7

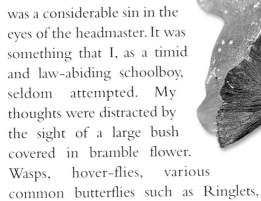

Photo 2: A Purple Hairstreak. (Wingspan 28mm); they usually settle with their wings closed. The hind-wings are silver-grey with a distinct white line (the hairstreak). Photo x1.8

was a considerable sin in the eyes of the headmaster. It was something that I, as a timid and law-abiding schoolboy, seldom attempted. My thoughts were distracted by the sight of a large bush covered in bramble flower. Wasps, hover-flies, various common butterflies such as Ringlets, Gatekeepers, Meadow Browns, Holly Blues and Small Coppers were jostling for places to feast off the nectar. In the midst of this melee, I saw two small unfamiliar tailed butterflies. The tall Cothill elm trees, and the W markings on the hind-wings made it clear that we had found the elusive White-letter Hairstreak. Very soon the butterflies were to disappear from this site – Dutch Elm disease caused the death of all the breeding elms, the Hairstreaks scattered (I saw them the next year in all sorts of unlikely places) and many colonies were eliminated.

Photos 3–4: Black Hairstreak pupa and butterfly. The chrysalis, and that of the closely related White-letter Hairstreak are often very visible on the upper side of their foodplant. The Black Hairstreak is a very shy butterfly, and is difficult to see even in places where there are known to be strong colonies. (Pupa 9.5mm; Butterfly hind-wing 16mm). Photos x2.

A few years later, enjoying a brief lunch-break in some Oxfordshire woodland, I found myself standing by a sloe hedge with an object that looked like a bird-dropping. I had found a Black Hairstreak chrysalis! In a hot summer, this stage of the life-cycle may last a fortnight, in a wet one it may last four weeks. In wet years, the disguise wears thin and it is estimated that up to four-fifths may be eaten by birds. In dry warm years, there is a much bigger rate of survival. The butterfly is hard to find, and if you want to see it, consult

3

4

Photos 5: Brown Hairstreak butterfly (Butterfly hind-wing 20mm, wingspan 40mm). Photo x1.5

B.B O.N.T. (Berks, Bucks and Oxfordshire Natural History Society) for advice about sites.

Professor Ford, of All Souls College, Oxford, author of *Butterflies* – a ground-breaking book first published by Collins in 1945 – whose experiments on the Scarlet Tiger Moth made the Cothill Marshes famous, entertained us to tea, and gave me a lot of help. He told me of a field on the edge of Bernwood Forest where he had seen all five British Hairstreaks, and advised looking for the Brown Hairstreak rather later in the year than is usually recommended in the books. One sunlit afternoon in late August, I was wandering down a wide ride in Bernwood, when I saw some giant hogweed plants some 50 metres ahead. Even at that distance, I was aware of a brilliant golden–orange butterfly feeding on the flower heads. As I drew closer, the female Brown Hairstreak continued her peregrination around the flower heads. Occasionally, she opened her wings displaying the brilliant orange bar that brightens her dark chocolate forewings. The female Brown Hairstreak, very unusually, is much brighter and more visible than the male. The males spent much of their time waiting in the 'master tree' (see chapter 4). Females can sometimes be seen crawling through sloe hedges, looking for safe places to lay their eggs. The bright white eggs, always laid in the fork of a branch, are easier to find than the butterfly! The first sighting of the Brown Hairstreak, and later the extraordinary contrast with its dull dead-looking chrysalis, spoke to me of the resurrection.

Theologically, my encounter with the White-letter Hairstreak was the most profound of the five. Breaking the headmaster's cardinal rule was trivial (though distinctly painful if you were unlucky enough to get caught), but my reaction was typical of human attitude to sin. Having acquired just enough courage to break the rule once, I repeated the sin on the same day! It all suddenly seemed so simple. Sin is like that, we quickly acquire a taste for it whether it be drugs, sex, financial chicanery, lying, exaggeration, pride or covetousness. St Paul makes this point very clearly when discussing his discovery of the commandment against coveting (see Romans 7). If caterpillars are endemically selfish and survival orientated, mankind is endemically sinful. A lonely cross outside the city wall of Jerusalem may seem a thousand miles away from a nervous schoolboy breaking bounds, but there lies the only remedy for our sinful nature. A caterpillar, by luck and good management, has a small statistical chance of becoming a butterfly; we have no chance of becoming spiritual butterflies, except by the grace of God

Photo 6: White-Letter Hairstreak butterfly (hind-wing 15mm). Photo x2

and the forgiveness of Jesus Christ. Inspired by a Green Hairstreak, thrilled by a dazzling purple one, fascinated by the brilliant camouflage of the black, given resurrection thoughts by the brilliance of the brown, it fell to the White-letter Hairstreak to forcibly remind me that my nature was, and to some extent still is, in a fearsome rebellion against God. Dickens's selfish, indolent Harold Skimpole may admire and desire the freedom of butterflies; but he uses their freedom as an excuse to sponge off his friends. He stands in a long line of nature lovers who want freedom without any sense of responsibility. The Christian gospel requires us to understand the bad news before we can properly receive the good!

Admirals and Emperors in a Sombre Wood
(Inner Healing)

*"Not Heaven itself upon the past has power;
but what has been, has been, and I have had my hour."*

(Dryden, from translation of Horace)

The Poplar Admiral is one of Europe's largest butterflies. Size, dark upper wings, and fast gliding flight differentiate it from other forest butterflies. It is usually discovered either drinking from a muddy puddle, or sunning itself on a sun-flecked forest track. When feeding, the butterfly displays beautiful hind-wings, which are a glorious combination of orange and white, encircled by an ice-blue band, which enriches the lower edge of its underside. As with many Nymphalidae (brush footed butterflies), the males are more frequently seen than the females. The male often feeds directly from the damp stones of forest paths, apparently absorbing salts which are necessary to make them sexually mature. At other times, he will open his dark wings to receive heat from the sun's rays; this raises his body temperature, which is essential if he is to fly. When disturbed, the male Poplar Admiral will either take no notice at all (he is far too busy engaged in the serious business of eating and drinking) or else he will soar upwards into the forest canopy. Then he can resume his search for an unmated female who may have recently emerged from her chrysalis.

Photo 1: Poplar Admiral Underside (hind-wings 40mm). Photo x1.2

In June 1997, we visited a sombre forest north of Verdun. We had been told about this forest by one of my most reliable entomological friends, who assured me that he had seen lots of Purple Emperors, Large Tortoiseshells, Poplar Admirals and even Large Coppers.

The weather was terrible there; we drove through pouring rain, stayed in a typically excellent small French hotel on the edge of the forest, and were relieved to find that the clouds had lifted by the following morning. Even so, it was scarcely a 'butterfly' day. We walked for some time down forest paths with scarcely an insect in sight. Just before midday, the sky cleared, the sun came out and our luck changed: we discovered the hidden butterfly track that my friend had told me about. Originally, this had been an ancient railway track running due south to Verdun some 30 kilometres away. It had evidently been built by the Germans to take troops and supplies to one of the First World War's bloodiest battle sites. A nearby German cemetery confirmed this. The track started a little way in from the forest road. It was overlooked by a curious bridge, which seemed strangely out of place in such a peaceful forest. The whole forest seemed quite eerie, as if the tragic fighting of 80 years earlier was still casting a malign shadow. White Admirals were flying in abundance, and other common forest species flitted along the track. Eventually, I found a way up to the bridge, and started to scan the canopy of the wood. Almost immediately, a great dark butterfly flew out of the tree tops, and descended to the path below. A few minutes later, I was very pleased to find the male Poplar Admiral still feeding on the path just below the bridge. Photography failed, as it had done on my only previous meeting with this butterfly in Croatia, and the insect flew off leaving me exhilarated by the sighting, but disconsolate at another photographic failure. Time was running out, and I thought it might be many years before such a photographic opportunity reoccurred. Then to my huge delight, the great black butterfly returned, and started feeding at exactly the same spot from which I had disturbed him. This time I tried a different tactic, I approached him with my large black nylon net. Quickly he was detained, boxed, and left under the shade of an aspen tree while we had some lunch. After about 20 minutes, I released him very cautiously in the shade of some bushes, which marked the edge of the path. The next 20 minutes were pure heaven! Our former captive remained completely docile, resting with wings both open and closed. He even walked up proffered branches of trees, and crowned it all by allowing another group of enthusiasts to video him. Eventually, I encouraged our former detainee to fly off. He soared, briefly, before descending to the same patch of muddy gravel, and resuming his interrupted feed!

Just over a week later, we revisited the forest. The sun was out and the butterflies were flying, but it was obvious that the weather was closing in. I returned to the bridge. From this excellent vantage point, I watched the White Admirals feeding on the bramble blossom beside the track, I noticed Lesser Purple Emperors (both the normal white form and the lovely yellow clytie form) flying around the tree-tops and along the bridge. Bridges are marvellous places for watching Lesser Purple Emperors, many times I have looked down over rivers and seen them flying beneath me. Walking to the other end of my vantage point, I looked down and saw, directly below me, a male Purple Emperor basking in the pale sunlight. All four wings flushed with the glorious iridescent purple which is usually so hard to see.

Despite this, I felt quite sad, and started to reflect about the railway track, which some 80 years earlier had been built to help the German war effort. Its purpose, I imagine, was to ferry troops and munitions to Verdun, one of the many bloody battlefields of the First World War. How did anyone survive its horrors? How were the survivors, and their descendants, scarred? It is hard enough in the natural cycle for a butterfly to survive. The Admirals and the Emperors have a similar strategy for winter survival. These species all hibernate as small caterpillars, relying on a mixture of wondrous camouflage and tent-making to get through nature's darkest time.

But what of the young German soldiers – how had they survived? How many had been driven unwillingly down this forest track towards a premature death in the hand-to-hand fighting that marked the bitter conflict around and within

Photos 2–5: White Admiral eggs, first instar caterpillar eating honeysuckle in the characteristic way, over-wintering caterpillar in hibernaculum – a cleverly spun tent which gives much needed protection (compare with photograph in chapter 11 of Purple Emperor caterpillar which hibernates in the open but changes the colour of its skin to match the surrounding bark of the tree on which it is resting). Fully grown caterpillar now camouflaged for spring (natural size eggs height 1mm, caterpillars 2mm, 5mm, 27mm – see also the first photographs in chapter 2 for completion of life-cycle).

Verdun? What of the many on both sides of that most dreadful conflict, whose faith in humanity and in God was so irrevocably dented, and often destroyed, by what they saw and experienced? Did the Poplar Admiral have a mystical message for them and for others trying to cope with the deep inner hurts which are so often part of life's tapestry?

The Poplar Admiral's glorious underwings (hence the name Iceblue used by some old German writers), conceals its sombre, almost black forewings. Many people seem to behave like the Poplar Admiral. Too often, I have taken the funeral of a war veteran, and his sorrowing widow has said to me, 'He would never talk about his wartime experiences – they were too painful.' Frequently in today's unhappy society people try to forget the traumas of their past. Rejection, abuse, bullying in childhood and at school, failed marriages, and many other bitter and unfortunate experiences leave people incredibly wounded and vulnerable. Most of the time they present a calm, relaxed appearance, enjoying all the normal pleasures of life – but inwardly in many hearts there is deep pain, often concealed and driven inward. Outwardly, like the beautiful Poplar Admiral displaying its closed wings, they seem at peace. But there usually comes a time when they need to open up and to receive counsel and healing prayer, to help overcome the present wounds caused by a traumatic past.

This is quite different from conversion (see chapter 1); it

usually occurs when people discover that the freedom in Christ for which they have hoped and prayed for, after conversion, hasn't completely taken place. St Paul presents the ideal in Romans 6:4 – 'we were buried therefore with him (Christ) by baptism into death'; but the ideal is seldom experienced. Many Christians, though wonderfully converted, carry deep hurts from their past which mar the freedom of their 'new lives in Christ'.

Just as the dark butterfly in the sombre wood needs the rays of the sun to lift itself back to the sky, so many individuals need to experience what the prophet and the hymn-writer (note 1) describe as 'the Sun of Righteousness risen with healing in his wings'. Many people are healed, and transformed by such a healing, both of past memories, and of the false guilt which so often accompanies these traumas. The soldier questions why he has survived, and the victims of abuse often feel (quite wrongly) that they are in some way to blame. Far too many people, including long-standing Christians, feel worthless. This despite the clear teaching of Scripture in Psalm 139 that God knows us all, intimately, and the great text from 1 Corinthians 6:20 – 'you were bought at a price'. I remember well a timid, lovely, clergyman who told me how his confidence was destroyed when as a teenager he was told that he was adopted and therefore unwanted by his natural parents. Most people who suffer from sexual abuse (and there are an appalling number) feel guilty, unclean and unworthy. Somehow they feel both partly responsible for their suffering, and unable to forgive their abusers. The simple words of the Lord's Prayer, 'forgive us our trespasses as we forgive those who trespass against us', seem impossibly hard to say.

Frequently, I have taken people to the words of St Paul in Romans 6:11 – 'In the same way, count yourselves dead to sin but alive to God in Christ Jesus'. The theology is (and I am greatly indebted to the wonderful Chinese Christian Watchman Nee [note 2]) that we cannot of ourselves forgive these terrible hurts; but if we are truly dead to ourselves and alive in Christ then he can forgive. Corrie Ten Boom (note 3) gives a wonderful example of this when she had been

Photo 6: The sombre Upper Wings of the Male Poplar Admiral (wingspan 80mm). Photo x1.5

reluctantly speaking about forgiveness shortly after the Second World War. She had been imprisoned; her father and sister had died for helping Jewish people escape from wartime Holland. After her talk, a German (whom she recognised as a particularly brutal SS officer in her wartime camp) came to ask for her forgiveness. He said that he had become a Christian since the war. She felt totally unable to forgive him, in complete contradiction to the message that she had been preaching. In desperation, she cried out to God for help, and felt a warm current travel into her arms, so that she was able to take the man and embrace him.

'Jesus Christ is the same yesterday and today, and for ever' (Hebrews 13:8) and he can stand at the hurts of all our pasts, and minister healing to the most traumatised of memories. This may well be a lengthy process requiring counselling or psychiatric skills, but often the Lord brings healing wonderfully quickly. Jesus said, 'I have come that they may have life, and have it to the full' (John 10:10) – and he meant it! But we are unlikely to have abundant life unless the painful memories of the past have been truly healed and the pain

Photos 7–13:
(opposite). Some of the butterflies which can be seen in and around the forest near Verdun:

7: Large Copper (wingspan 40mm). This butterfly became extinct in England when the marshes in the fen country were drained.It has been re-introduced and survives precariously in Wood Walton Fen near Huntingdon. Near the Damvilliers forest, it flourishes in some marsh land.

8–10: Map butterfly, spring and summer forms (wingspan 35mm). The dramatic difference between the spring and summer forms also occurs in some African butterflies. Slight differences occur in other European butterflies such as the Comma and the Holly Blue.

11–13: Lesser Purple Emperor (Female underside, female clytie [yellow] form, male, male clytie form feeding, wingspan 70mm).

erased. The memories will remain, but we will remember the events without the overwhelming feelings of hurt, anger, false guilt and rejection. It makes little difference whether it is the awful violence of war, or the domestic violence of home or school. It makes little difference whether we are the innocent victims or the guilty perpetrators (and often one becomes the other). We all need to be set free.

'You will know the truth, and the truth will set you free' (John 8:32) is another of Jesus' great promises. When the male Poplar Admiral basks with his dark wings fully open on the warm stones of a forest path, this is essential for his well-being. In our case, we need to honestly face our dark pasts in the light of Jesus' love and grace. This may be hard, but it is much safer than pretending to look beautifully composed with our 'wings' tightly closed. Then, and perhaps only then, we shall experience fully the true radiance of Christ's healing love. When we are healed, we will be better able to serve others in his needy world. We shall understand what the saintly Bishop Ken (note 4) meant when he wrote:

'Forgive me, Lord for thy dear Son, the ill that I this day have done, That with the world, myself, and thee, I ere, I sleep at peace may be.'

Notes
1. From verse 2 of 'Hark the herald-angels sing', which is based on Malachi 4:2.
2. Watchman Nee, *Sit, Walk, Stand* (Kingsway, 1962), p. 18.
3. Corrie Ten Boom, *Tramp for the Lord* (Hodder and Stoughton, 1974), p. 75.
4. Thomas Ken in the hymn 'Glory to thee my God this night'.

7

8

9

10

11

12

13

CHAPTER 7

The Mourning Cloak
(Bereavement)

"Why do you always wear black?"
"I am in mourning for my life. I am unhappy."
(Anton Chekhov, *The Seagull*, Act 1,
Masha replying to Medvienko)

Outside Bath Crematorium, I was waiting for the mourners to arrive. A middle-aged couple came up to me, and admired the orange tip butterfly embroidered on my purple stole. A poignant conversation took place (as they often do in such surroundings). They told me how they often visited their son's grave in the cemetery at Chamonix. He had, I think, been killed in an accident on the mountains above. The mother remarked, 'We nearly always see a Camberwell Beauty flying around the grave – it gives us great hope.'

The Camberwell Beauty was first recorded in England in 1748 flying around some willow trees in Cold Arbour Lane, in what was then the village of Camberwell. Other British naturalists, thrilled to see a butterfly which was known to be a very rare migrant, came up with the more romantic name 'The Grand Surprise'. The butterfly is even rarer in Ireland. The great Victorian naturalist South records that on one occasion it was seen 'settled on the roadside in County Tyrone. It was not captured, the day being Sunday!'

In Germany, Scandinavia and North America it has been given the much more solemn name Mourning Cloak – derived from the drab colouring of its hind-wings which, being dark brown reticulated with black, remind many watchers of mourning crêpe.

The butterfly flies over a huge range of territory. It can be found in much of Europe: from the forests of Finland near the Arctic Circle to northern Spain, and across Eastern Europe and temperate Asia. A rather more gaudily coloured sub-species is often seen in North America. After hibernation, the golden colour on the borders of its wings fades to white; but

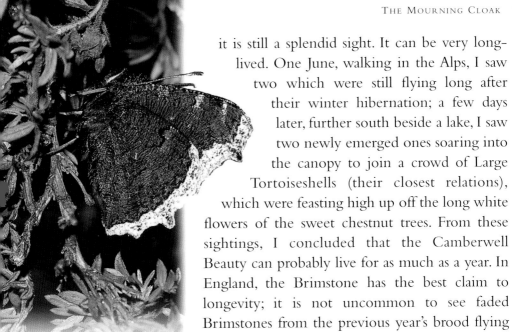

Photo 1: The Camberwell Beauty, resting near the Tour du Pin in Languedoc, showing the dark funereal markings of its underside (hind-wing 36mm). Photo lifesize

it is still a splendid sight. It can be very long-lived. One June, walking in the Alps, I saw two which were still flying long after their winter hibernation; a few days later, further south beside a lake, I saw two newly emerged ones soaring into the canopy to join a crowd of Large Tortoiseshells (their closest relations), which were feasting high up off the long white flowers of the sweet chestnut trees. From these sightings, I concluded that the Camberwell Beauty can probably live for as much as a year. In England, the Brimstone has the best claim to longevity; it is not uncommon to see faded Brimstones from the previous year's brood flying with their successors.

Over the years, I have found the Camberwell Beauty a most elusive butterfly. My first two sightings were in the late summer. The first was when stopping for a cup of tea in a dark Austrian forest. One appeared, swooped three times around our car, flashed the golden edges of its wings in the gloom of the woodland, and then, tantalisingly, disappeared. The second, fully fifteen years later, was beside a minor French road in the Massif Centrale. We had just escaped from one of those monumental French traffic jams, and were speeding along a straight minor road at about 100kph. I noticed a large field of thistles, obviously full of butterflies – presumably mainly Graylings. Near the roadside, something distinctive and different caught my eye. I ground the car to the halt, ignored the protests of the family, and made them all pile out! We walked back about 100 metres to observe a wonderfully pristine Camberwell Beauty, resplendent with maroon flecked with bright purple-blue spots and glorious gold edges to its perfectly formed wings. It fed off the thistles for a few minutes, before retreating into the forest, exactly when I returned from the car with the camera! Even the children were impressed, and turned the incident to their advantage at our silver-wedding party a few years later.

In its prime before hibernation, the Camberwell Beauty is

Photo 2: The Camberwell Beauty, or Grand Surprise, in its full glory (wingspan 74mm). Photo lifesize

usually seen flying at great speed down forest tracks, its golden-edged wings flashing in the sunlight. The butterfly has a distinct liking for fruit, and can sometimes be seen gorging itself off over-ripe pears or apples. A Polish friend of mine achieved a beautiful photograph after leaving a suitably large pile of rotting apples outside his forest home. Hibernation usually takes place in cold mountainous places – maybe this is why the rare British immigrants are seldom seen the following spring and have never been known to breed in England.

During hibernation, the Mourning Cloak's sombre underside provides protective camouflage and obviously helps its survival in a dangerous period of its life-cycle. As the days lengthen, and the spring sunshine encourages the buds on the breeding trees to open, the butterfly reappears and heads down from the mountains to the warmer valleys. Like our familiar Peacocks, Small Tortoiseshells and Commas, it mates in the spring. After courtship flight, the female then heads for the side of a small stream, and looks for a suitable willow (or further north a birch tree), on which to lay one or several amazing bracelets, eventually releasing up to 500 eggs. (See chapter 10 for a photograph of the very similar Large Tortoiseshell eggs.)

I have had many more sightings of the butterfly in the spring. Typically, it is seen basking on paths, or resting on warm open ground. When disturbed, which is fatally easy for the would-be photographer, it usually returns to the same place. Nevertheless, from my limited viewing it certainly justifies its more romantic name of the Grand Surprise.

Both sexes seem to live for quite a long time after mating. The caterpillars grow up gregariously, before dispersing to pupate. A friend of mine, on his honeymoon, driving up a steep hill in the Black Forest (in Germany) noticed a sallow bush that seemed to have been stripped of most of its leaves. A quick stop, and a large number of caterpillars were spotted, some of which were abducted. They pupated noisily the next night in the confines of a waste-paper basket topped with nylon which his long-suffering bride had bought in the local market.

Photo 3: A Camberwell Beauty chrysalis (length 25mm). Photo x1.5

It is quite strange that such a beautiful butterfly has become associated, by name at least, with death and mourning. It is somehow characteristic that much of humanity should name the insect after its drab underside rather than its glorious upper wings. My opening quotation from the inexorably gloomy play *The Seagull* rather underlines this.

The experience of mourning is something that few of us can avoid. It is hardest when experienced unexpectedly. But even when death is expected, the grief of husbands, wives, parents, children or friends can be overwhelming. My sharpest experience of bereavement was when my mother died, quite young, after early heart surgery. I was just starting at theological college. Despite her strong faith, and my absolute confidence in the resurrection of Jesus, the whole process was one of a deep, numbing pain. The complete desolation experienced by my father, who had a much less secure faith, added to the trauma. For me, there were the unanswered theological questions. My grief was considerably lessened on the night of my mother's funeral when I read the familiar words in John 16:20 – 'You will grieve, but your grief will turn to joy'. These words spoke like an arrow into my heart – they contained a promise, and the next few verses amplified that promise in a very specific way which eventually was fulfilled.

A typical site, spring-time beside the River Endre in Var in southern France, with suitable trees for the Camberwell Beauty to lay her eggs. Also included in the photograph are other spring butterflies found there (a) Spanish Festoon (wingspan 45mm); (b) Southern Festoon (wingspan 52mm) – the Festoons have just four European species. They lay their eggs on Birthwort, and are amongst the brightest of the spring butterflies in southern Europe; (c) Moroccan Orange Tip (hind-wing 20mm); (d) Nettle Tree Butterfly (hind-wing 22mm) – an unusual butterfly with very long palpi (the sensory organs either side of the tongue). It is the only European member of the family Libytheidae which has only about ten members worldwide. (e) Long-tailed Blue (hind-wing 18mm); (f) Southern White Admiral, which sometimes flies with the White Admiral (wingspan 54mm). Photos x1.5, x1.5, x2, x2, x2, x1.2

I was fortunate that my grief was overarched by a strong faith that 'Death has been swallowed up in victory' (1 Corinthians 15:54). Looking back, I could have made much better use of my mother's last few months. There were many things that we could, and should, have talked about. That is another of the great problems of approaching bereavement. How much does one talk about death? It is particularly difficult when the outcome of a particular illness is still unclear. When death comes, it seems so final, and can easily be made much worse by unnecessary guilt and the haunting feeling of 'if only'. Faith cannot protect us from the ravages of death. C. S. Lewis (note 1) expressed this eloquently in his book *A Grief Observed*. He writes:

> It is hard to have patience with people who say 'There is no death' or 'Death doesn't matter'. There is death. And whatever is, matters. And whatever happens has consequences, and it and they are irrevocable and irreversible.

Lewis's grief was made worse by the hopes and false dawns that he had about his wife's cancer. But at least they were able to talk. Almost her last words, said to the chaplain at the hospital, were 'I am at peace with God'.

It has been a great privilege to be with people as death approaches, and a greater one still to be with someone at the actual moment of death. If people have the time (not always granted) and the courage (not always available) to talk about death, eternity and the future for those left behind, the whole process of dying can be quite beautiful. The faith of some people, despite being in great pain, is truly remarkable. I think of a nurse, who in earlier life had been riddled with strange fears, approaching a painful death with a radiant faith that astonished all her visitors. I think of the twinkling eyes of a senior clergyman, who having summoned me from my Sunday lunch because he was sure that he was dying, responded graciously to the reading of a few verses of a psalm, then closed his eyes and asked to be helped to move back onto his bed. He died almost immediately afterwards. There was a great sense of quiet faith and dignity as he crossed what Bunyan in

A typical Alpine butterfly site where we saw the Apollo, the Camberwell Beauty and the Poplar Admiral on the same day in June.

that wonderful part at the end of *Pilgrim's Progress* calls 'the river of death'. Such memories will always stay with me. A friend (note 2) has an even more poignant story. She writes:

> *Ruth had been my Director of Studies when I was a student. She inhabited a square, chaos-filled room with a big window overlooking the sunlit grass of the college quadrangle. Pictures produced by her school-age children hung crookedly on the walls; books and papers were piled high on the desk; and stimulus and encouragement oozed out of the brickwork for those who reached the mark of her high standards. I had spent many hours there breathing it all in, and she had changed me. After graduation, I stayed on to do research, and saw her less often. But one day, I was told as I walked back from the library back to my college for lunch, that her cancer had returned. Over the next few months I was to spend many hours with her again, shorter visits this time, sharing the jokes I'd picked up from my fellow researchers at lunch time, and watching her die. As I found myself forced to face the fact that this was what was going to happen, the universe that I had so carefully constructed for myself fell apart. I was an atheist and an existentialist, believing that there was no meaning to life except that which we create for ourselves. Ruth was a Catholic and a Christian, and whilst I ran to my doctor for something to alleviate my stress, she prepared for death with the calm and matter-of-factness of someone packing their bags for a long vacation. I asked her about it. The Christian faith, she explained, had provided a meaningful framework for life for people in all kinds of societies and cultures over a period of two thousand years. Could I, she asked, imagine my late 20th-century philosophy making sense to a 13th-century peasant? Of course I couldn't. She died at Easter, and the day before she died she presented me with a beautifully illustrated Book of Hours. In it she had written, in Latin, 'I know two masters, Christ and Letters'. Within a matter of weeks, so did I.*

Without faith, bereavement is much worse. There is no real hope. People adopt a number of strategies, with varying degrees of success. For the mourner faced with the terrible pain of the death of a friend, companion, partner or child, there are various tactics. In years gone by, excessive solemnity marked by the wearing of dark mourning clothes, or widow's weeds, was the expected custom. Nowadays, a more up-beat strategy is in favour. Often this involves the virtual denial of what has taken place. 'Fred has passed away'; 'Death is nothing at all' (the beginning of a disastrous soliloquy composed by a distinguished cleric and often read at funerals). This sanitisation of death is often accompanied by unrealistic memories: 'We never had a cross word'; 'He was such a perfect husband, wonderful father…'. Theologically many people like to hide behind a vague optimism: 'There must be something beyond'. Sometimes there is stark unbelief: 'Let's have a good party and celebrate Percy's life (which is what he would have wanted)'. Occasionally there is a jest based on the now popular belief in reincarnation: 'Let's hope Hugh doesn't return as a wasp'; or more often words which express the reasonable thought that 'Iris's life continues in her children and grandchildren'.

There are four main beliefs about the future life. For the atheist, and most agnostics, death is final. The deceased person's life can be celebrated, remembered and enjoyed. There is a brave finality in such a view, and some cope well. For many, there is a sort of vague universal optimism: 'It's all right for Dave – he'll be up there playing better golf than he ever managed on earth'. This belief, almost totally unjustified in Scripture, is the most difficult one for the believer to confront. For many from Eastern faiths, there is an expectation of some form of reincarnation. I have written elsewhere why I feel that this position is untrue (note 3). The traditional Christian view expressed by Paul that 'the dead in Christ will rise first' (1 Thessalonians 4:16) gives the only realistic hope.

At this stage, it would be good to think again about our butterfly. The life-cycle of The Mourning Cloak offers an interesting and hopeful avenue of thought. Our long-lived butterfly passes through three adult phases: First there is the summer period of emergence, care-free flying and imbibing nectar – preparation for the cold winter that lies ahead. Then there is the period of dark desolate hibernation, which leads on to the third and most useful stage. In the spring, our butterfly awakes, finds a partner, and if female, then searches with great care for a suitable tree on which to lay her eggs.

Many of us pass through these stages. For much of life we are relatively carefree. If we are wise we are preparing for whatever winter may bring. Time spent studying the faith, and experiencing the warmth of believing will prepare us for our particular winter. If this winter takes the form of bereavement, there will be a period of shock, isolation and grief, during which few others will be able to help us. When spring comes, we reawaken ready, and perhaps better equipped, to fulfil our calling in Christ's world. I have known many bereaved people, and divorced ones as well, who after a period of mourning have risen to greater acts of service than they ever achieved before. Sometimes, those who have experienced the deepest tragedies are given special grace which enables them to help others in similar circumstances. Psalm 84, which describes a pilgrimage to Jerusalem, is particularly helpful. The journey becomes stifled by the arid Valley of Baca. Here the pilgrim can despair, turn back, attempt to scramble out of the valley, or if he is wise 'make it a place of springs (v 6)'. Water can be found by digging, and the pilgrim can be refreshed. Finally, he can join the sparrow and the swallow singing in the court of the Temple in Jerusalem.

Spiritual winter, whether caused by bereavement or other difficulties, always wants to give way to spring. Shakespeare writes of this in the opening line of *Richard the Third* – 'Now is the winter of our discontent made glorious summer by this sun of York'. We need to be realistic about our own, and other people's, depth of grief; but there will be a time when the solemn drab Mourning Cloak is laid aside and 'The Grand Surprise' arises to bask again in the bright sun and the promise of a fruitful spring-time.

Notes

1. C.S. Lewis, *A Grief Observed* (Faber and Faber, 1961), p. 16.
2. Dr Alison Morgan, author of various books including *The wild gospel: living by truth in a changing world* (Monarch 2004). Her testimony is also found in the introduction of that book. I, too, was glad to know Ruth as a friend and as a Godparent to her eldest son.
3. John Woolmer, *Healing and Deliverance* (Monarch, 1999), p. 276 ff.

Conservation Matters
(our God-given Responsibility)

What is man, that thou are mindful of him:
And the son of man, that thou visiteth him?
Thou madest him lower than the angels:
To crown him with glory and worship
Thou makest him to have dominion of the works of thy hands:
And thou hast put all things in subjection under his feet:
All sheep and oxen: yea, and all the beasts of the field:
The fowls of the air, and the fishes of the sea;
And whatsoever walketh through the paths of the seas.
O Lord our Governor: how excellent is thy Name in all the world!

(Psalm 8:4–9, Book of Common Prayer)

The opening chapters of Genesis teach many deep theological truths. They proclaim that there is a creator, that he 'saw all that he had made, and it was very good' (Genesis 1:31)', that mankind is *central to God's purposes*, that there is a spiritual opposition, that mankind rebelled and misused its God-given freedom, that there will be redemption when 'the seed of the woman bruises the heel of the serpent' (Genesis 3:16), and that mankind has been given responsibility to look after the earth, the sea and all that lives within them. 'Non-violent dominion' is a good phrase which others have used to describe the commands of Genesis 1:28–30.

James Jones, the Bishop of Liverpool (note 1), in his challenging book *Jesus and the earth* quotes from a poem 'To a Butterfly' written by William Wordsworth. The second verse reads:

Oh! pleasant, pleasant were the days,
The time, when, in our childish plays,
My sister Emmeline and I
Together chased the butterfly!
A very hunter did I rush
Upon the prey: – with leaps and springs

I followed on from brake to bush;
But she, God love her! Feared to brush
The dust from off its wings.

Bishop James makes the point that the poem captures our human ambivalence to creation. One child sees the capture of a butterfly as a challenge, the other reveres the insect, knowing that even to touch it is to risk damaging its fragile wings. He sees within most of us both attitudes – a self-indulgence which continues to widen the gap between need and greed, and a reverence which is captivated by the God-given beauty of his creation. The account of the creation, in the first three chapters of Genesis, tells us that God enjoyed his creativity. It is our privilege to share that enjoyment and our responsibility to help preserve every part of 'the work of God's hands' (Psalm 19:1).

Butterfly conservation is not a simple matter. It is far easier to destroy a habitat than to recreate one. 'Leaving it to nature' usually results in the spread of bushes like hawthorn which quickly stifle both the nectar and the breeding plants which butterflies need. Releasing vast numbers of artificially bred butterflies has no long-term impact. Butterfly conservation needs highly skilled people, who require considerable co-operation from land-owners. We shall look at a few encouraging stories, always bearing in mind that these are *exceptional*.

On 1 September 1971, I walked with Jane, who was then doing Voluntary Service Abroad, from Dogura on the coast of Papua New Guinea for some three hours inland. We crossed innumerable streams, wading through quite high water, walked beside the river through a butterfly paradise (the lovely Lacewings settled amidst the long grass, their fiery red wings edged with a brilliant purple sheen), past a great expanse of open water where several streams met and then watched the magnificent Mountain Blue Swallowtails skimming across the water. After that, we turned away from the river, and walked up a wide forest track. I had read, somewhere in the library at the Holy Name School at Dogura, that the Birdwing butterflies were often seen from the beginning of September. I read too, with some amazement, that the early missionaries, unable to catch them, used to collect them by shooting them (what would Wordsworth have made of that? Why didn't they ask the help of the locals who were able to catch them and use live insects as head-dresses or even as children's toys?). A little way down the track, a dark shadow crossed the path. I looked up, and drew breath: a male Birdwing was skimming through the forest canopy. His great forewings, spanning 140mm, were extended fully as he glided above the path displaying the electric green and black markings characteristic of the species. He flew high above us, but was easily visible, for some minutes. He then swooped into a tree, and emerged pursuing the far larger, and much darker, female.

One day soon, we expect to return to PNG and perhaps be privileged to see the even more beautiful, and larger, blue Birdwing – the Queen Alexandra. Birdwings, of which there are eleven species in PNG and West Irian, are closely protected (except for the most common species), and are a conservation symbol for the country, and something of a success story. For some species, the danger is from collecting (very high prices can be paid for perfect specimens of the rarer species); for others, there is an even greater danger from habitat destruction. All too often, natural trees have been hacked down to make way for ornamental pines and the like. However, a system of butterfly farming has been established. This process involves looking after the habitat, growing foodplants in either an organised or fairly random manner (the conservationists have now realised that random planting, while less easy to manage, looks much better and is preferred by the butterflies!), protecting as far as possible the caterpillars, collecting pupae while leaving half the stock to repopulate the farm and releasing many of the newly emerged butterflies. The result is that some pupae can be collected for butterfly houses throughout the world, some butterflies can be sold legally as specimens and some (more than would happen naturally) can be released back into the environment. The farmer gets a worthwhile income, the forest is preserved and habitats are both protected and improved – with the result

Photos 1–2: Male and Female Birdwings (hindwings 70mm and 95mm). Photographs with the help of Worldwide Butterflies, who have been involved in the conservation scheme described in this chapter. Photos lifesize

that the butterfly population is likely to increase or to remain stable. This is an unusual story, and a model of what could happen in other fast-diminishing rain forests throughout the world (note 2).

I have visited two majestic African rain forests, Kakamega

Photo 3: A member of the Sailor (Neptis) family resting on a coffee tree (wingspan 70mm). Ironically cash crops like coffee are a major cause of deforestation and loss of butterfly habitats. Photo lifesize, taken in Agaun, PNG.

in Kenya, and Bwindi in Uganda. Both these wonderful places are being well protected and managed. The tall hardwood trees of Kakamega give the forest a deeply mysterious presence. Part of the forest is surrounded by a huge tea plantation. This gives it much needed protection from nearby villagers who would come and destroy its trees. Good work is also done by the forestry commission which manages the whole area and grows seedlings of the forest trees. People come from afar to study the snakes (of which the cryptically coloured Gaboon Swamp Viper is the most feared). There is some attempt to farm the butterflies, but this appears to be much less advanced than the work that I have described in PNG. There is a great variety of habitat within the forest: grassy hilltops rising far above the canopy – the meeting place for many romantically inclined butterflies; wide-open tracks where monkeys, birds and butterflies can be seen in great numbers and the dark sinister forest full of trees which provide important medicinal cures. Deep within the forest, there are occasional sun-flecked parts of pathways where the shy and beautiful Euphaedra butterflies gather to feast off half-eaten figs dropped, from on high, by passing monkeys. These hidden places, perhaps no more than 30 metres of path and a few metres of undergrowth either side of the path, are a butterfly watcher's paradise.

The Impenetrable Forest near Bwindi in south-west Uganda is far larger, and of even greater significance. It is one of two places in Uganda where the mountain gorillas can be seen. The majestic woodland is home to many butterflies, birds, monkeys and snakes. The whole forest, which extends far across the border into both Congo and Rwanda, is well preserved, and brings much needed income from tourists who pay substantial sums to see the gorillas. It is also home to *Papilio Antimachus*, an orange-brown tailless swallowtail with a wingspan of up to 230mm – easily Africa's largest butterfly! Five of the most beautiful days of my life were spent walking near the eastern entrance and in the denser forest near the dangerous border with the Congo. The vehicle track was quite elevated, most of the tree canopy was far below and we could see many monkeys, apes and birds. We found bamboo strewn on the road, left in a way characteristic of mountain gorillas, we could hear large animals crashing around in the nearby thickets, and Jane and Susie almost certainly caught a glimpse of them, disappearing deeper into the forest. Great blue birds, Turacos, were flying by the water's edge; myriads of butterflies were feasting off animal dung (civet's droppings were particularly attractive!) and feeding from flowers along the forest paths. In places near water, dung or damp patches, the butterflies could be numbered in hundreds – occasionally in thousands (see chapter 2, photo 9). Deep in the forest, we caught glimpses of leaf butterflies (with dazzling upper wings which when closed give the butterfly such a convincing outline that you think you are being deceived into photographing a dead leaf), we found the Blue Diadem basking in a rare patch of sunlight, we encountered various species of Charaxes, with two or even three tails, hurtling up the pathways looking for females, and driving competitors, or blue-shirted rivals like me, off the track. We met three varieties of Red Admiral, some tailed, and all flying near their breeding plant – a type of large nettle with a particularly vicious sting. We occasionally saw female Charaxes fluttering deep in the forest searching for their food plant on which to lay their eggs, and seeking to avoid the predatory males. The good news is that Bwindi has a serious conservation programme both for the protection of the Mountain Gorillas and the study of butterflies.

So far this chapter reads as if conservation is an unbridled success story – of course, it isn't! Throughout the world,

The forest floor deep within Kakamega. Euphaedra Preussi (wingspan 95mm), is feeding and around the edge of the photograph are some of the many other spectacular residents: (a) Euphraedra Preussi (the male is blue, the female is purple); (b) Euriphene Ribensis (male) – a particularly shy butterfly which occasionally rests to absorb some sunlight on its lovely wings (wingspan 50mm); (c) Rattray's Forester feeding off a fig probably dropped by a monkey hind-wing 45mm); (d) Cymothoe Lurida (Lurid Glider wingspan 80mm). (e) Common Forester (wingspan 60mm). The Mother of Pearl (see Chapter 11) is another beautiful resident of the forest. Photography here is a little hazardous, apart from the possibility of disturbing snakes, kneeling on the forest floor leaves one very vulnerable to safari ants! Katy, then aged 11, was a brilliant catcher of butterflies. It is impossible to identify many species without first catching them.

The forest canopy in Bwindi: including inserts of some of the many beautiful butterflies which we saw during a visit to our daughter Susie. In 1998, she taught in a local school under the auspices of the Right Hand Trust. (a) Blue Mother of Pearl (wingspan 90mm) – this brilliant butterfly can be very common in some forests; (b) Blue Diadem, a shy butterfly that it was a great thrill to meet deep in the forest (wingspan 110mm); (c) Kallima Cymodoce, which looks just like a leaf when its dazzling forewings are closed (wingspan 70mm); (d) White barred Charaxes (hind-wing 52mm) – a typical two-tailed member of the family. Different members of the Charaxes family can sometimes be found in groups of 20, or even 50, queuing beside animal dung; (e) Acraea Semivitrea (wingspan 60mm). The Acraeids are a slow-flying family of butterflies, most of them are highly toxic to birds, as their caterpillars feed on plants containing cyanide compounds. Consequentially other species mimic them to gain protection. Photos all approximately lifesize

deforestation is rampant, smaller pieces of woodland are being devastated, wild animals have virtually disappeared except from game reserves, and even there they are still in danger from poachers or angry villagers whose livelihood can easily be destroyed by a herd of marauding elephants. The situation varies throughout the world, and is far worse in the Amazon basin where huge tracts of rainforest disappear every day. But at least there are some successes. Chaos theory says a little flippantly that one butterfly flapping its wings in South America can trigger a hurricane in Africa. This may or may not be true, but what is true is that if local villagers realise the value of the butterfly, both ecologically and commercially, there will be far more attempts to preserve the forests, and the consequences for both local and global welfare will be considerable. The butterfly is quite an indicator as to what is happening ecologically in the wider world.

Much of my butterfly watching has been in Europe, and here the problems for butterflies in particular, and conservation in general, are much more complex. European species such as the Apollo and the Marsh Fritillary are closely protected; but as elsewhere habitat destruction, draining of marshes and use of pesticides are the main problems. The practice of 'set aside' doesn't appear to help. Former agricultural land quickly becomes a tangle of unhelpful plants in which no self-respecting caterpillar would want to grow up. There are, as you would expect, dramatic contrasts. A large deciduous forest in the foothills of the Pyrenees with wide, butterfly-friendly paths, is virtually without insects; but a huge wood north of Verdun (see chapter 6) has many rare species. Not far from the first wood, a hillside with a little sallow yields courting Purple Emperors and rough ground on a different hillside yields a flourishing colony of Large Blues which fly even in the rain!

In Europe, there is always the excitement of stumbling across old-fashioned meadows, full of wild flowers, not overrun by scrubland bushes, and free from pesticides. Many come to mind: one was a meadow north-east of Figeac, in central France, which we found by deviating from a main road. It was quite small, perhaps half a hectare in area, surrounded by trees, brambles, and full of flowers. I think in one brief hour, which was all the time we had, I counted about 50 different species, including the Niobe Fritillary which I hadn't previously identified. Photography was impossible — you couldn't move towards one butterfly without disturbing a dozen others which in turn disturbed the one you were stalking, but it was an enchanted meadow. Ominously, there was a small vineyard across the road; I wonder if the field has survived. The foothills, and lower levels of the Alps and other mountain ranges, can also provide marvellous habitats. Finding a good butterfly site requires patience, luck, and an entomological sixth sense!

Photo 4: Chequered Skipper (hind-wing 14mm) – this butterfly became extinct in England, although there are reports of reintroductions in Lincolnshire; but it flourishes in some parts of north-west Scotland.
Photo x2

Mountainous areas seem less encroached, and British rarities like the Chequered Skipper can be quite common in the woods of the Alps and of the Pyrenees. One word of warning: good sites can disappear overnight, and can never be replaced. I received an unpleasant surprise when I returned to a site in southern France where I had seen Camberwell Beauties in some numbers, only to discover that their basking ground had been enclosed and usurped by horses.

There are many natural habitats left in France, Spain, Austria, Poland and other European countries, and maybe the limited reforms of the Common Agricultural Policy will help to prevent the spread of useless agricultural expansion. When we turn to Britain, the situation is still more complicated and yet more hopeful. In our over-crowded island waste-land is always disappearing; for instance, heath-land with fine colonies of Silver Studded Blues regularly gets sold for building. Yet natural recovery and specialised conservation efforts are helping some species survive and even flourish. Overall however, the record is still one of continuous and dangerous decline.

Two species, the Comma and the White Admiral, have managed to increase their range, and their numbers. The Comma, a Victorian rarity which would send collectors in

Photographed on or near the sedum-covered slopes at Allons, on the edge of the French Alps: (a) an Apollo caterpillar (length 50mm) found with great difficulty after clambering the slopes on Ascension Day 1996; (b) Apollo (hind-wing 42mm); the Apollo is found on many mountain slopes in Europe. It has very thinly scaled wings, characteristic of very primitive butterflies, and can still be found in large numbers at suitable sites. It is closely protected in most of Europe. (c) Duke of Burgundy (hind-wing 16mm); this butterfly is the only European member of the family Nemeobiidae which has many members in the American tropics, and a few in Asia and Africa; (d) Arran Brown (wingspan 54mm). It was reported to exist on the Isle of Arran, but this doubtful record has never been confirmed; (e) Striped Grayling (hind-wing 31mm).The Graylings are a large family of butterflies, which usually rest with their wings closed, and angled to the sun in such a way as to minimise the length of their shadow. This peaceful hillside, far from the madding crowd, was one of our happiest discoveries!

Photos 5–6: Upper and undersides of the Comma (wingspan 48mm). The Comma hibernates in the open, its white 'comma' marking the only visible part as it rests against a tree-trunk.
Photos lifesize and x2

droves by train to Herefordshire, is now found, and easily seen, over the whole of Wales, southern England and the Midlands. No simple explanation has been found (nor for the comparable decline to the point of extinction of the Large Tortoiseshell which some Victorian collectors thought sufficiently common as to be scarcely worth recording when found feeding on thistles in the wooded regions of southern England).

The White Admiral, too, has achieved a remarkable expansion of the number of places where it can be seen. Very rare in the second half of the nineteenth century, it is now steadily moving west and north. The less good news is that the drift northward is further evidence of the effect of global warming. The White Admiral, who lays her eggs on honeysuckle, seems to prefer woods which are growing darker and more shaded, whereas most other woodland species need light and space. Thus as this species flourishes, others decline.

The case of the Pearl-bordered Fritillary is much less encouraging. In the middle of the nineteenth century, it could be found in the clearings of almost any wood in England, Scotland or Wales. Now it is almost confined to the south-west of England, Wales, the Lake District and in a few areas of Scotland. The reason for its decline is a change in the management of woodland. The Pearl-bordered Fritillary depends, for its very survival, on woods being coppiced. Coppicing which involved cutting down an area of woodland and clearing the scrub, allowed the breeding plants – various sorts of violet – to flourish. I have watched a large colony of Pearl-bordered Fritillaries courting, mating and laying eggs in a sunny clearing in a wood in south Gloucestershire. The glade was carpeted with bugle, primroses, violets and other woodland flowers. The butterflies enjoyed the sun, drank nectar from bugle and other flowers, and were easily seen to be laying their eggs on the violets. But if that clearing became over-grown, and if there wasn't another suitable one nearby, the next generation of butterflies would decline in numbers, and soon the colony would become extinct.

Space precludes discussing other British species. Sadly most of our Fritillaries are in steep decline, and are found in a small number of suitable habitats mainly in the south–west or north–west of England.

Theologically, it is tempting to draw parallels with the decline (or growth) of churches. For suitable habitat, read joyful welcoming churches, which feed people. For availability of breeding plants, read effective and imaginative evangelism. For insecticides, read materialism, pornography or anything else that dulls the soul and shuts out the still small voice of God. For reintroductions of butterflies like the Large Blue (see the next

Photos 7–9: Pearl-bordered Fritillary (hind-wing 23mm) feeding in a typical woodland clearing; High Brown Fritillary (hind-wing 31mm) is now found almost exclusively in the west of England; Heath Fritillary (female above the male – wingspans 44 and 40mms) which survives in Kent and the south-west of England thanks to intense conservation efforts by many organisations including the Duchy of Cornwall.

Typical Garden Butterflies include: (a) Peacock (wingspan 58mm – lays its eggs on nettles in sunny places especially beside streams); (b) Speckled Wood (wingspan 50mm – this shade-loving butterfly breeds on grasses and has several generations each year); (c) Orange Tip (wingspan 46mm – the females have grey tips to their wings, the butterfly lays her eggs on jack by the hedge, ladies' smock, and some garden plants like sweet rocket. The bright orange eggs are easy to find, and should be collected if there are more than one on a plant as the caterpillars are cannibalistic; (d) Wall Brown (wingspan 46mm – eggs are laid on grasses); (e) Gatekeeper (wingspan 40mm – eggs are laid deep in grass; note the prominent scent brand across the wings showing that the butterfly is male; (f) Large Skipper (wingspan 33mm; note the moth-like posture with wings half-open, which is typical of many members of the Skipper genus, and the male scent brand prominent on the forewing); (g) Grayling (hind-wing 30mm) which is mainly a butterfly of our chalk hills; (h) Meadow Brown (male-wingspan 50mm). Other very common garden butterflies include Small Tortoiseshell, Red Admiral, Painted Lady, Comma, Holly Blue, Common Blue, Brimstone, Small Copper and Brimstone (all illustrated elsewhere); and Small Heath, Green-veined White (which is not a pest) together with the unpopular Large and Small Whites which lay their eggs on cabbages and other garden plants.

chapter), read church-planting. But this would be to travel down an attractive but dangerous by-way.

The Christian church, especially if it takes seriously Jesus' teaching about the kingdom, must make strenuous efforts to promote conservation, and to help look after the planet. We cannot leave such an important matter to New Age thinkers, Friends of the Earth, and the anti GM crops lobby.

One place, where each of us can help both conservation (and church growth) is in the use of our homes and gardens. The humblest garden can be home to many butterflies especially if breeding plants, as well as nectar-bearing plants, are available – long grass left for the Speckled Wood, docks for the Small Copper, nettles in a sunlit (!) patch for Small Tortoiseshells and Peacocks, nettles in the shade for Red Admirals, Holly and Ivy for the Holly Blue.... In the same way, a friendly use of the home for church groups, for parties, as open house for troubled neighbours, can do wonders within a community. In rural England, and in small towns, the local church is one of the few places where true community living is still experienced.

Conservation is a kingdom issue. In the wilderness, Mark records that 'Jesus was with the wild animals, and angels attended him' (Mark 1:13). Jesus, in the midst of his first recorded battle with the powers of darkness, is in perfect harmony with creation. Jesus spoke much about creation, he understood the importance of creation, and he used many aspects of creation to illustrate his message. We may not understand how 'the leopard will lie down with the goat' (Isaiah 11:6); but it is our responsibility to make sure that both survive until the end of time as we now know it.

Notes

1. James Jones, *Jesus and the Earth* (SPCK, 2003).
2. Michael Parsons, *The Butterflies of Papua New Guinea* (Academic Press, 1999) p. 67 ff which includes the interesting quote (p. 77) 'Butterfly farming is becoming recognized as an alternative income to clearing the rain forests'.

CHAPTER 9

Unlikely Allies
(The Good Samaritan)

"There never was a King like Soloman
Not since the world began;
But Soloman talked to a butterfly
As a man would talk to a man."
(Rudyard Kipling, *The Butterfly that stamped*)

L ooking for caterpillars is a fairly unrewarding task for the amateur naturalist; a few species are relatively easy to find, most are remarkably well camouflaged. Gardeners know all about Cabbage White caterpillars (which also enjoy chomping nasturtiums); most of us have seen nests of Small Tortoiseshell and/or Peacock caterpillars usually in large clumps of nettles in open ground – preferably near water. Over the years, I have found Orange Tip caterpillars on jack by the hedge, Red Admiral caterpillars in their conspicuous tents made of nettles, Brown Hairstreak caterpillars in the midst of sloe bushes (a big surprise – but the two I found were on the move and their bright green bodies, which are normally well camouflaged, were easy to see as they moved on the stem of the sloe bush which was their home). My greatest discovery was made on a hot afternoon in the south of France. In quick succession, I found three virtually fully grown caterpillars of the Two-tailed Pasha, sunning themselves amidst strands of white silk which flashed in the sunlight, as they basked on the upper-leaves of their food-plant – the wild strawberry tree (see insert on p. 58 which gives the complete life-cycle of this butterfly). This large bush, whose berries when ripe make excellent jam, grows prolifically in the scrubland and woods about 50 miles from the Mediterranean coastline. Like others, I have found it easy to find butterfly eggs – usually by the simple expedient of watching the female laying; and, strangely, the very small larvae of the first instar. These tiny larvae often eat in a very distinctive way – often sitting on the stem of a leaf which they have substantially demolished. White Admirals, Purple Emperors, Two-Tailed Pashas, amongst others, are relatively easy to find at this early stage of their caterpillar life.

One sunny morning in May, we were having a picnic on chalk-downland near the White Horse at Bratton in Wiltshire. I was hoping to see the elusive Duke of Burgundy, the Green Hairstreak, and possibly an early Adonis Blue. We were sitting on a bank, surrounded by horse-shoe vetch and other chalk-loving flowers. I don't know whether I saw the ants or the caterpillar first, but I became aware of a large greenish-blue caterpillar, shaped like an overgrown wood-louse, lumbering through the grass, attended by about four ants. Experienced entomologists know this sight well – the Adonis Blue caterpillar with a small platoon of ants in constant attendance. In this situation, there is a mutual benefit. The ants get well fed, licking sugary substances off the caterpillar's body, and in return they give the caterpillar a measure of protection from predators. They even take the caterpillar into their nests at night, let it pupate in the warmth and safety of their chambers and, most surprisingly of all, attend the emergence of the butterfly from the chrysalis.

Photo1: Adonis Blue Caterpillar (length 15mm) with attendant ants. Photo x2

This amazing symbiosis is common amongst the Lycaenidae (that is the Blues, the Coppers and the Hairstreaks) and takes place in different ways for different species. For some like the Green, Brown, and Purple Hairstreaks it is thought that the ants just protect the chrysalis which apparently can 'sing' to attract the attention of helpful ants! For caterpillars of the Black and White-letter Hairstreaks which pupate on leaves there appears to be no protection – they are too high up for the ants to reach them.

There is one extraordinary exception to this rule of mutual benefit. For years no one could farm the caterpillars of the Maculinea family (five species in Europe including the famous Large Blue). It is easy to see the Large Blue laying on wild thyme (or marjoram in many sites in Europe); and eventually the small first instar caterpillar will eat its way out of the egg shell, and start to feed on the thyme. But any attempt to keep it in captivity always ended in failure! In the autumn, after completing some initial skin changes, the caterpillars always died when kept in captivity. This was a huge puzzle to Victorian naturalists who particularly prized the Large Blue on account of its beauty, and the small number of places that it was found in England. Captain Purefoy, about 100 years ago, solved one of entomology's greatest riddles. Observing some Large Blue caterpillars feeding, he was amazed to see the tiny caterpillar drop off its food plant. It was then climbed over first by one red ant, and then by up to a dozen others which were attracted to the scene.

Eventually, Captain Purefoy and others worked out what was happening. The small caterpillar somehow attracted the ant, which then tapped the caterpillar causing it to discharge a minute drop of liquid from its honey gland. After other ants had been attracted, and then left the scene, the original ant spent quite a time with the caterpillar. The caterpillar, which looks remarkably like an ant grub, now even acts the part, rearing up and making its body taut like that of an ant grub. The ant then captures the caterpillar in its jaws, and takes its prize back into the nest amongst the brood of grubs. Here, the caterpillar adopts a new diet, eating its way through a thousand or more ant grubs! Its weight increases a hundredfold, and this remarkable 'cuckoo' hibernates for the winter, resuming feeding in the spring. Most do not survive, having either run out of food, or because their disguise has been rumbled. It is generally felt that only caterpillars adopted into the larger nests survive, and that if a nest has more than one adopted caterpillar then none survive. If they are successful, they pupate in the nest, and when ready to emerge, the butterfly with its small crumpled wings is accompanied by a bevy of protective ants!

This butterfly became extinct in England in 1979 – probably due to myxomatosis, the disease which decimated the rabbit population in the 1950s. The rabbits maintained a close-cropped turf, which kept the ground temperature high enough for the red ants to flourish. Once the rabbits were not abundant enough to keep the grass short, the ants started to decline in numbers, and the butterfly was doomed. A similar species from Sweden has been introduced to various nature reserves in the south west of England. On the site that I visited, the colony was so flourishing that the project managers wanted to remove females from the site because they feared there would be too many caterpillars waiting to be adopted; and that, in the end, most would starve!

I have seen this butterfly in many parts of Europe, particularly in the Alps, quite high up above Chamonix, in the Pyrenees, in Languedoc, and most of all in the Valley of the River Lot. Here in 2001, it was so numerous that it could be seen along roadside verges. Its headquarters seemed to be a large rough field full of marjoram. There was no sign of any rabbits to keep the vegetation down, but presumably the ground temperature was so much higher in central France that the ants could flourish without their assistance. There certainly seemed to be plenty of ant nests, and the butterflies could even be found on roadside verges. The relationship between rabbits, ants and butterflies affects other species – such as the Adonis Blue. One Wiltshire site was being grazed by sheep imported to do the job of the rabbits! Adonis Blue populations seem to have increased since this approach was adopted. All of this may help to explain why conservation is such a complex measure. The naive idea of releasing adult butterflies and waiting to see what happens is usually doomed to failure.

Photos 2–4: The Large Blue (wingspan 43mm) in England, in central France, and a typical site in France – an uncut field full of marjoram and ants nests.

Photos 5–9:
Butterflies whose caterpillars are protected by ants: (5,6) Adonis Blue (wingspan 34mm) – male and dark coloured female near her breeding plant which is horseshoe vetch. Note the dark veins which break up the white margins at the edge of the wings which is a distinguishing characteristic of this species; (7) Brown Argus (wingspan 29mm) with a touch of iridescent purple sheen on the dark brown wings; (8) Common Blue (wingspan 35mm) – the photograph shows a female with black-blue colouration, she can take a variety of forms ranging from blue to black. All of these can be distinguished from the male by the orange spots at the edge of the wings; (9) Small, or Little, Blue (wingspan 25mm – the smallest British butterfly). A female on her food plant, kidney vetch, – see also chapter 2, photo 14.

The positive relationship between ants and most members of the Lycaenidae family of butterflies takes most people by surprise. Jesus did just the same with his most famous parable.

Asked by a lawyer the leading question 'Who is my neighbour?', he replied with a simple but extraordinary story:

A man was going down from Jerusalem to Jericho, when he fell into the hands of robbers. They stripped him of his clothes, beat him and went away, leaving him half-dead. A priest happened to be going down the same road, and when he saw the man, he passed by on the other side. So too, a Levite, when he came to the place and saw him, passed by on the other side. But a Samaritan, as he travelled, came where the man was; and when he saw him, he took pity on him. He went to him and bandaged his wounds, pouring on oil and wine. Then he put the man on his own donkey, brought him to an inn and took care of him. The next day he took out two silver coins and gave them to the innkeeper. 'Look after him,' he said, 'and when I return, I will reimburse you for any extra expense you may have.'

Which of these three do you think was a neighbour to the man who fell into the hands of the robbers?

The expert in the law replied, 'The one who had mercy on him.' Jesus told him, 'Go and do likewise.'

(Luke 10: 30–40)

We cannot fully understand this story without appreciating the extent of the strained relationships between the Jews and their near neighbours the Samaritans. The Samaritans were descendants of a population returned to Samaria, after the Assyrians had sacked the city of Samaria and deported most of the population. The Assyrians replaced the original population with different races, who had different religions and little understanding of the Jewish faith. Years later, the remaining Jewish tribes were deported by the Babylonians, but they didn't practise this form of ethnic cleansing, and these Jewish people were returned to their homeland by a Persian king who had defeated the Babylonians.

Jesus told the parable as a reminder of our common humanity, and to teach us that doing good is not meant to be confined to our friends, family and co-religionists! His disciples certainly needed the lesson. A little earlier in his Gospel, Luke records that James and John had wanted Jesus to call fire down from heaven to destroy a village in Samaria which had failed to welcome them!

Christians today are challenged to be good neighbours in a wide variety of situations. All around me in Leicester, there are people working hard to help refugees, while some of the population wishes they had never arrived on our shores. We have many opportunities to obey Jesus' teaching. In my last parish, a group of people worked very hard to set up and to maintain a house for homeless young people. Hardly any of them asked the church for spiritual help or had any apparent interest in what we believed, but they were grateful for the shelter and other assistance that they received. We were called to be 'good Samaritans' to them.

If ants and Lycaenidae caterpillars can support one

Photo 10: Chalkhill Blue (wingspan 36mm). The photograph is of a typical silvery-blue coloured male. Chalkhill Blues can be seen in huge numbers on some downlands. Like the Adonis Blue they breed on horseshoe vetch. They have only one late summer generation, while the Adonis Blue has two – in May–June and late summer. The Chalkhill Blue is another butterfly which gains protection from its relationship with ants. Photo x1.5

another, then the lesson for us is not only about unconditional giving but also about learning to receive. Jesus' parable would have been much less shocking if it had been a Samaritan who was attacked and a Jew had come to help him. But we have to remember that there will be situations when we desperately need the help of others of different faiths and racial background. In the Second World War, many Jewish people learnt that lesson, some receiving help from non-Jews in the appalling situations in which they found themselves. I am not sure that we can draw any parallels from the one-sided relationship between the red ants and the Large Blue caterpillars, except to be aware that it is possible for Christians to behave with that sort of supreme selfishness, and that we need to be alert to our own motives, and to be sure of the genuineness of our offers of help!

The parable of the good Samaritan has inspired many unselfish acts, not least the efforts of those called Samaritans, who sit at the end of telephones to counsel people in the depths of suicidal despair. Much of nature is very cruel, and caterpillars have many predators; the relationship between some ants and the Lycaenidae caterpillars makes for a welcome change.

Isaiah has an extraordinary vision of a future when 'the wolf will live with the lamb' (Isaiah 11:6). How this can be is impossible to foresee; but in the meantime we are called to learn from nature, and much more importantly from Jesus' parable, that mutual help and support to and from other people is a vital part of making the world a better place. My Muslim neighbour and I may never reach a religious consensus, but we can treat one another as brothers and help to set a better example. If ants and caterpillars can achieve this, we ought to be able to do rather better!

CHAPTER 10

The Large Tortoiseshell and the Hornet

(Spiritual Warfare)

"Will you walk into my parlour?" said a spider to a fly.

(Mary Howitt)

Photos 1–4: Large Tortoiseshell eggs (height 0.8mm), caterpillar (length 45mm), chrysalis (length 25mm), butterfly (wingspan 70mm)

I was standing in the shade of a wood near Uzes in the south of France. I looked up and saw several large dark orange butterflies flapping uncertainly through the trees. My heart missed a beat – surely these were the elusive Large Tortoiseshells? This butterfly, very rare or more probably extinct in England, was one that I particularly wanted to see. The unusual quantity of the butterflies, and their hesitant flight, suggested that they had just emerged from the chrysalis. Large Tortoiseshell caterpillars, like Peacocks, Small Tortoiseshells and many others, live in massive webs – only

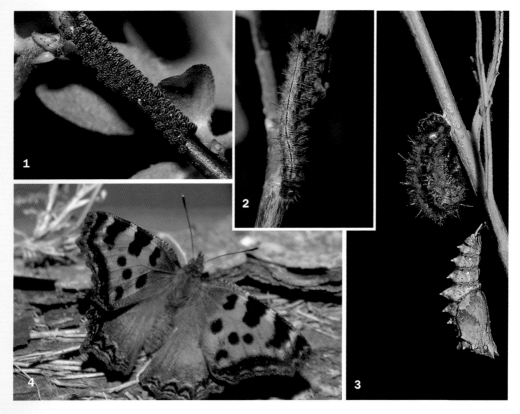

Photo 5: Red Admiral (wingspan 70mm – note that it has an enemy lurking beside it. On this occasion the spider was unsuccessful!) Photo x1.4

dispersing to find somewhere to pupate. We noticed several butterflies sitting on the branch of an elm tree, opening and closing their wings as if preparing for their first flight. Nearby, on the main trunk of the same tree, I saw one basking with its wings fully open. It was resting beside a clump of ivy – perhaps that was where the chrysalis case now lay empty. It looked very beautiful, even from a considerable distance.

Then disaster struck. A hornet flew into the wood and, as if guided by radar, made straight for the butterfly, sat astride its body, and pierced the butterfly's wings with its strong legs. Four fragile wings, each punctured by the hornet, fluttered down at our feet. Moments later, I noticed another Tortoiseshell had taken up position on the same trunk, sitting adjacent to the hornet. Would it, too, be killed and then devoured? Jane and I threw small stones at the tree trunk. Eventually, Jane scored a hit on the tree trunk just below the insects. Butterfly and hornet flew off in opposite directions. I was reminded of the words of Jude 23 – 'snatch others from the fire and save them'. Words famously applied by John Wesley to describe his escape, when he was plucked, when very young, by his formidable mother from a fire in his father's rectory.

That night, in our camp site, we witnessed a role reversal. For several days, a Red Admiral had seemed to live in our rectangle of space, which was surrounded by flowering privet hedges and mulberry trees. Each evening, it came to sit on the roof of our car, and was greeted with cries of 'Butbee, Ad, Ad,' from an enthusiastic Rachel (then aged two). That night, a hornet flew menacingly across its territory. With an angry flick of its big black and scarlet wings, our Red Admiral took off, and flew round and round the hornet. The hornet, somewhat alarmed, turned and sought its supper elsewhere.

It seemed to me we had just witnessed a rather good illustration of the words of St Peter: 'Be sober, be watchful. Your adversary the devil prowls around like a roaring lion, seeking someone to devour. Resist him, firm in your faith' (1 Peter 5:8,9, RSV). All the butterflies had experienced the miracle of rebirth; but one of the Large Tortoiseshells hadn't had quite the faith to fly, and had been cut down by the hornet before it could be of any use. The Red Admiral, confident and mature, coped quite easily with the assault of its hornet.

Many years later, in May 1998, I witnessed the outcome of another, rather more subtle battle. Every year, I watched for Holly Blues, who would cruise through our garden, heading for the large holly tree which dominated one end of the churchyard. Most years, I would see a small number, but in 1998 there was a population explosion. Often I could see as many as a dozen at one time; it was easy to find eggs, and even tiny caterpillars, on the buds of the holly flowers. I captured a few females, and then released them after they had laid some eggs. I farmed about a dozen caterpillars, protecting them and feeding them. Most days, I would pick a small amount of holly to feed my captives. One day, I noticed a small wasp with a long ovipositor, lurking on the branch that I had picked. I easily identified it as a parasitic wasp, Listrodomus Nycthemerus, which flourishes by piercing Holly Blue caterpillars with its ovipositor and then injecting its own eggs into the doomed caterpillar. Adult wasps emerge from up to 90 percent of the pupae of what otherwise would have been emerging Holly Blue butterflies.

6

Photos 6–7: Holly Blue caterpillar on ivy (length 13mm) and butterfly (wingspan 35mm) – a female of the summer generation which has striking black markings on the edge of its wings. The summer generation lays its eggs mainly on ivy, the spring one mainly on holly. Photo x1.3

That year, I had just started to write a book called *Healing and Deliverance*, and I was wrestling with the question as to whether in some places, and at some times, dark spiritual forces can grow so strong in a region that they can stifle any effective Christian witness. The Lord seemed to give me a spiritual interpretation of the Holly Blue phenomenon. 'Today's church is largely built up by the families of believers, carefully farmed and protected from the worst of the world, just as your caterpillars were protected by you. If you want an explosion of new members, you will need to defeat the spiritual powers which are targeting your church and locality, just as the Holly Blue numbers explode in the rare years when the parasitic wasp is largely unavailable to sting the vast majority of caterpillars.'

The Holly Blue butterflies only have exceptional years if for a period of time the wasps have been largely absent, and in the same way Christian evangelism sometimes depends on defeating the relevant spiritual powers. In order to help build up the numbers in any colony of this butterfly you will need to see a substantial reduction in the numbers of its dangerous parasite. In the same way, particular spiritual powers target and control particular regions, and you may need to identify them, and through the cross (see Colossians 2:15) announce their defeat. Such tactics have allowed real progress in a number of regions (note 1), and I have seen, and described elsewhere, a battle of some significance in the remote village of Mutwe Wa Nkoko (the village of the severed chicken's head) in northern Zambia. The parable of the sower, a key parable about evangelism, teaches us that in normal circumstances spiritual growth is impeded in a variety of ways which include the immediate destruction of the seed by the birds of the air. Accounts of spiritual warfare in various parts of the world suggest that, in exceptional circumstances, dark powers may prevent any real spiritual progress – until they are identified, challenged and defeated. The Holly Blue cycle could be used as a butterfly parable pointing to that kind of situation, while many other butterflies have less subtle and more obvious enemies. The attack by parasitic wasps on the Holly Blue, and some other species, passes largely unnoticed, but it is a thorough and deadly process. The spectacular attacks by birds, dragonflies, hornets and wasps on adult butterflies are much more noticeable but perhaps statistically less significant. Christian leaders are well aware of Satan's attacks on themselves and their flock. They know all too well that some Christians are effectively disarmed before their discipleship has really begun, and that other more mature Christians are disabled by serious sin, doubts and spiritual exhaustion. Of course, no analogy is completely satisfactory, and mercifully through repentance and the receiving of God's grace we can be restored, whereas the unfortunate caterpillar or butterfly has no second chance! But we seem to be largely unaware of how Satan, like the ichneumon wasp stinging a caterpillar, effectively ensnares much of the population. Just as different wasps target different species of caterpillar, so Satan has completely different tactics in different places. In remote rural Zambia, belief in and the practice of witchcraft, fear of ancestors, initiation rights for youngsters and the like disarm many people spiritually. During my last visit to Zambia, a very old lady asked two of my team to pray for her release from evil spirits. She knew they had entered many years earlier when she had attended some teenage initiation rites. After a short prayer, her face was wreathed in smiles, and she felt much clearer about her discipleship. A few years earlier in this same remote village, near the Angolan-Congo border, two of my team heard an evil spirit speak through someone they were praying for – *in perfect English*. By contrast, in African towns and cities, the scourge of AIDs and the consequent break-up of families cause much misery and create many very different spiritual problems. In Europe, it is our comfortable lifestyle, affluence and general lack of spiritual awareness which seem to be our deadliest spiritual foes. It is much easier to see butterfly predators picking butterflies off one by one; but the defeat of the parasitic wasps has a far greater effect on numbers. Of course, things can get out of control, and if numbers increase too much then the food supply is exhausted!

Spiritually, most theologians would agree about the dangers to individuals, but are far more cautious about full-scale spiritual warfare as practised by evangelists in South America, Asia and Africa. Perhaps we need to learn a lesson from the largely unseen attacks of the most dangerous butterfly predators!

Studying the ichneumon fly (or wasp) leads me to attempt to answer a very awkward question: *'How can we believe in a God of love when nature is so obviously red in tooth and claw? Why is nature so beautiful, and yet so full of pain?'* It is very easy to marvel at the gratuitous beauty of nature. The very structure of a butterfly wing, with its amazing scales arranged like an elaborate mosaic of coloured roofing tiles, the glorious colours – some obtained by natural pigments, some by light refraction – don't serve any obvious evolutionary purpose. There is some evidence that male butterflies (and some birds) are favoured by females if they have the brightest colours.

Some butterflies look very different at different times of the year. Others, like our Holly Blue, exhibit minor differences in successive generations. Again, there is no obvious reason for this.

But these gentle speculations can soon get overtaken with much darker forebodings. On the wider canvas, we can watch in horror at mankind's selfish destruction of the ozone layer,

8

Photos 8–9: Close-up of wings of living butterflies (Blue Mother of Pearl with some iridescent colouring, and Citrus Swallowtail).

9

rain forests, fishing stocks...the list is endless. But even in the world of butterflies, there are many problems. We have looked in chapter 8 at the wider issue of conservation, and the relentless destruction of butterfly habitats in many parts of the world. We considered some of the many predators faced by the fragile butterfly at all stages of its life-cycle. Even their tiny eggs are far from safe. Attempting to photograph the egg of the Two Tailed-Pasha, I was quietly attempting to focus through my extended camera lens, when a small lizard

Photos 10–12: Gaudy Commodore dry (wingspan 60mm), wet (50mm), and intermediate (60mm) forms. It is unclear why some butterflies, notably the Map in Europe (see chapter 8), and many species in Africa have dramatically different wing colouration according to the time of year when the butterflies hatch. The Gaudy Commodore defies all logic, these photographs were actually taken on the same day in Uganda. I have also seen the wet and dry season forms of this butterfly flying together in Zambia!

appeared, stuck out its long tongue, and then disappeared with its lunch-time snack. I think the most savage predators are the various forms of ichneumons. Even eggs are vulnerable to some species, but they mainly attack caterpillars. Ichneumons also lurk beside pupating caterpillars – waiting to sting the newly formed chrysalis before its outer case hardens. The Marsh Fritillary has a particularly sadistic enemy – the apalantes wasp. Each generation of caterpillars is potentially a host to three generations of the wasp. Newly hatched caterpillars, found in large communal webs, are attacked in July. The parasites remain inside their hosts until August, and then leave to spin their own cocoons. The second generation wasps sting the medium-sized fourth larval stage of the marsh fritillary – they over-winter inside their hosts. Infected caterpillars die in the spring, the parasites emerge, form cocoons, and the third generation of wasps is ready to sting the final stage of the caterpillar cycle. They then put a sort of time delay into their hosts, so that the caterpillars slow down, and the wasps don't have to form their cocoons too soon. At this stage their cocoons are particularly well encased in silk, and the adult wasps don't bite their way out for four to six weeks. This second time delay gives surviving caterpillars time to have pupated, the adult butterflies to have

Photos 13–17: egg mass (height 0.8mm); caterpillars, in the spring, basking on their food plant (length of larvae 7mm); chrysalis (length 21mm) of Marsh Fritillary; Marsh Fritillaries pairing; caterpillar of Moroccan Orange Tip with cocoons of a parasite attached.

emerged, eggs to have been laid, and means that a new generation of small caterpillars are ready for attack! Just once I found a Marsh Fritillary caterpillar, fully grown wandering around the site at Bratton, at the same time as the butterflies were flying. Surprised, I took it home. Within a few days, the skin of the caterpillar was covered with white cocoons. I had found an example of the apalantes wasp's clever time delay in action! One entomologist, Jeremy Thomas, estimates that in some years three out of every four caterpillars are killed by these parasites, but that there are years when the parasite has a hard time (particularly when there is a cool but sunny spring). These weather conditions enable the caterpillars to develop too fast for the parasites and there is a much higher survival rate – which of course can have a knock-on effect into the next year. He estimates that in a good year (for the

butterfly) parasites only afflict ten percent of the caterpillars. If this happens for several years in succession numbers can build up quite dramatically.

At this point, we can make a number of theological choices. We can join Professor Dawkins, an eloquent and persuasive apostle of atheism, and agree that evolution does not require a creator. Indeed, we may agree that the evidence of an in-built selfish gene points decisively against such a possibility. The atheist/agnostic can make a very strong case. Most Christians are reduced to replying with personal testimonies of special revelation – from Scripture, in prayer, from visions and other direct encounters with the unseen world, through external signs such as healing, deliverance, guidance and protection. More surprisingly (see chapter 6), experiences of God are found in the midst of suffering and when experiencing grace through other people's suffering. From a different perspective, some will be able to make a strong case for belief in God by sifting the evidence for the resurrection (see chapter 11), or from an individual's experience of conversion (see chapter 1).

However, others will be willing to tackle the issue head on. Even allowing for the dark side of nature, we can argue that the overall beauty of creation is so great, that we can live with the mystery of the suffering and the brutality. St Paul hints at this when he writes (Romans 8:19–20):

> *The creation waits in eager expectation for the sons of God to be revealed. For the creation was subjected to frustration, not by its own choice, but by the will of the one who subjected it, in hope that the creation itself will be liberated from its bondage to decay and brought into the glorious freedom of the children of God.*

Isaiah in a great vision foresees that (Isaiah 11: 6–9):

> *The wolf will live with the lamb, the leopard will lie down with the goat … the infant will play near the hole of the cobra, and the young child will put his hand into the viper's nest. They will neither harm nor destroy on all my holy mountain, for the earth will be full of the knowledge of the Lord as the waters cover the sea.*

That will be the time when the whole of creation will be redeemed and restored.

There is another line of argument. We can, and I believe we should, argue that creativity involves the taking of risks. The creator could have set up a clockwork universe which didn't involve growth or decay, joy or pain, eating and being eaten, chance or planning. Such a universe would be monotonous, and leave little room for real quality of life. If we all lived for ever on this earth, there would soon be no room, little food, and a strange lack of freedom. If no caterpillars were destroyed, there would soon be far too many butterflies.

It is now time to consider the main question. Can a good all-loving God really have created, by whatever means, something as unpleasant as the ichneumon wasp? Christians naturally turn to the book of Job. This majestic poem (whether read literally or allegorically) introduces us to a man who, although overwhelmed by calamities and surrounded by useless advisors, is at last allowed to meet God face to face. In essence God humbles Job with a simple question: 'Where were you when I laid the earth's foundation?' (Job 38:4).

This unanswerable question is followed up with a tour of creation, including some of its most destructive members – lions and their prey (Job 38:39); the hawk and the eagle whose young ones feast on blood (Job 39:30). The speech also

Photo 18: Another battle – a spider builds a web to catch a Comma butterfly when it emerges from the chrysalis attached to our garden fence. I went on holiday, and didn't witness the outcome. A cow, in the field on the other side of the fence, destroyed the spider's web just before we left. But, on return, there was no trace of an empty chrysalis, and the spider was back in position. I concluded that the spider had won a somewhat unequal contest. (Pupa length 21mm). Photo x2.4

includes some of the victims like the ostrich (Job 39:13–18) who lays her eggs on the ground unmindful that some wild animal may trample on them! Ultimately Job is covered with very proper confusion, and realises that his knowledge, like ours, is totally inadequate for understanding these mysteries. Mystery is indeed inbuilt into the heartbeat of the universe. Job finally speaks some wise words: 'My ears had heard of you but now my eyes have seen you. Therefore I despise myself and repent in dust and ashes' (Job 42:5–6).

I think that we might say, and God's answer to Job points us in that direction, that the freedom and beauty of one butterfly far outweighs the destruction of a hundred caterpillars. The ichneumon fly is also a creature of strange wonder, and it, and other butterfly predators have a right to live. Our question is too anthropomorphic, and far too sentimental. We saw earlier (chapter 5) that Dickens's foolish character Harold Skimpole thought that he had a divine right to sponge on others, and that he cheerfully misused the concept of a butterfly's freedom to his own potential advantage; perhaps we have as little right to question our creator's judgement because we find parts of creation gruesome, sadistic and unattractive. Creation is very beautiful, deeply mysterious and often brutally harsh. Life for mankind is not that different – but curiously it is African Christians beset by the ravages of HIV, malaria, water-borne diseases, poverty and low life expectancy, who are often much more cheerful than their philosophising counterparts in the West.

We would do better to gaze at the subtlety of the checks and balances within the wonderful system, and to accept that death is now inbuilt into the universe. This is a mystery that, with faith, we can accept. Indeed, with so many enemies, the truly amazing thing is that any butterfly of any species survives. Sadly, the butterfly's greatest enemy is neither birds nor parasites, but mankind. It is the destruction of habitat, (even as I write a tractor is going past our house bent on cutting some long grass which is housing lots of Meadow Browns, Skippers, Small Heaths and Common Blues – butterflies which may one day become rare if we treat their natural habitat with such disdain) coupled with the climate

Photo 19: A female Marsh Fritillary. Her body was so weighed down by her egg supply that she was unable to fly (wingspan 48mm).The photograph was taken on a dull day when I took a rather reluctant Susie and Tim on a butterfly expedition. It has been used by the World Wild Life Fund to remind people that this once common butterfly is now an endangered species in both UK and Europe. Photo x1.7

change caused by global warming, and the all pervasive use of insecticides, that really threatens the survival of each butterfly species. Even then, we can marvel at their ability to adapt. A rare species, like the Black Hairstreak when faced with the destruction of its blackthorn hedges in Surrey, managed to redeploy to a nearby disused railway line and flourish. The Marsh Fritillary, much endangered in the British Isles and Europe, has lost many of its wetland habitats, but is making a limited recovery on chalk-hills where its food plant (the devil's bit scabious) also flourishes!

Isaiah writes of God who says unequivocally (Isaiah 45:7): *'I form the light and create darkness, I bring prosperity and create disaster.'* These powerful words, recorded by a great prophet, should stop us from being over-sentimental about creation and may properly bring our chapter to a close.

Note

1. See especially C. Wagner, *Warfare Prayer* (Monarch, 1992), and other writings by the same author, and *Healing and Deliverance* (*op. cit.*, p. 38ff).

CHAPTER 11

The Grandest Surprise
(The Resurrection)

Flashing among dark woods and their laughter. The butterflies!
Auburn air-thin glittering velvets and gauzes are flying –
Holy with happiness, shining with Heaven's light.
(Edith Sitwell, *Butterfly Wealth*)

For many centuries, the perfect newly-emerged butterfly has been used as a symbol of hope for mankind's longing for an afterlife. The contrast between the dark, virtually motionless, chrysalis and the brilliance of the newly emerged insect can be breathtaking. During the course of ten days' serious photography for the Tanzanian National Parks Association in the Arusha National Park, we had seen a Gold Banded Forester sunning itself on a log; its wings lit up by the low sunlight. The next day, I wandered into some vegetation near the path. The grasses were long, the Colobus monkeys were crashing around overhead, and the late afternoon sun was pouring, almost horizontally, bypassing the trunks of the tall trees. A few metres in front of me, another Gold Banded Forester was resting, wings fully open, its purple and golden colours sparkling in the sunlight. I dropped to the ground, and crawled cautiously towards one of the world's most beautiful butterflies. I hoped that I wouldn't encounter a snake, nor cross the path of the safari ants which frighten even elephants, and above all that my shadow wouldn't fall on the butterfly and cause it to fly away. Thirty seconds later, I had taken a short series of photographs, almost unable to hold the camera steady, as I took in the full beauty of a pristine butterfly

Photo 1: Gold Banded Forester (wingspan 70mm) in evening sunlight. Photo x1.1

with its iridescent wings displaying many glorious shades of purple and gold.

St Paul wrote, 'What no eye has seen, nor ear heard, nor the heart of man conceived, what God has prepared for those who love him' (1 Corinthians 2:9). These are majestic words which have inspired many people both during their earthly pilgrimage and at the point of death. His vision of paradise recorded in 2 Corinthians 12:1–10, and the experiences of others (note 1), have helped to encourage us that our spiritual journey is towards a great conclusion and that it is not just a facile delusion.

The transfiguration of Jesus (Luke 9: 28–36) was the most mystical incident recorded by the Gospel writers. The time of prayer, the presence of Moses and Elijah, the cloud, the voice of God, and the transformation of his clothing described as 'bright as a flash of lightning', combine majestically to fill us with awe and reverence.

While visiting the Luapula Province in Northern Zambia, I was preaching in the open air in the village of Mutwe Wa Nkoko. It was a beautiful day, and large blue butterflies were flying high up amidst the trees. Eventually, as I have written elsewhere (see chapter 10), the day became difficult, and it became obvious that many villagers were spiritually very bound by their associations with witch doctors. One woman, when being prayed for, even spoke to my wife and me in perfect Oxbridge English. She and others were controlled by powerful spirits. We had a difficult afternoon. The next day a local woman, not a known church leader, testified to having seen a figure dressed in white walking around the church in the half-light of dawn. Her face shone with a strange brilliance, and she and others were convinced that she had seen an angel. Our visit was transformed, and the local priest Father James has often spoken of the effect that the visit made on him and the village. Some years later, I visited World Wide Butterflies to ask if I could photograph a Blue Charaxes butterfly, similar to those I had seen on that day. I said to Robert Goodden, the founder and proprietor, 'You probably think that I'm mad, but I want to photograph the butterfly because in the same village someone saw an angel.' He smiled,

and said, 'My wife had her life saved by an angel on the A 303' (note 2).

The accounts of the first Easter Day are full of meetings with angels. Not surprisingly there is some confusion in the four Gospels as to how many angels, and figures dressed in white, were present. The presence of angels is neither surprising nor should be a cause for disbelief. Throughout the centuries, many people have had encounters with angels. Angels were key witnesses, and heralds, of the first Easter Day, and their presence adds to the power of the Gospel story.

But all this pales into insignificance when we consider the true meaning of the first Easter Day, and its consequences. If the biblical records are true, this was the most important day in the history of the world. The evidence from the Bible, from history, from individual spiritual encounters, and from the evident power of the name of Jesus is, to me, convincing and clear.

Many times, I and countless others have experienced how prayer in the name of Jesus has cleansed buildings and people from evil powers. Sometimes this has been so effective that people involved in the prayer have felt the force of the powers of darkness as they have left. Experiences like that make it much easier to believe that Jesus of Nazareth is indeed risen from the dead; and that just as he encouraged his first apostles with the promise 'And surely I am with you always, to the very end of the age' (Matthew 28:20), so he is present today when prayer is offered in faith and according to his will.

It was this power, and the presence of Jesus mainly through the Holy Spirit, that the first Christians relied upon to take their message into a sceptical and hostile world. Their message of Christ crucified and risen was most certainly 'a stumbling block to Jews and foolishness to Gentiles' (1 Corinthians 1:23).

The very first apostles, and some 500 of their followers, had the grandest surprise of all – they were met by the risen Lord! Saul of Tarsus on the road to Damascus had the most famous of all encounters – an encounter repeated in visions to a small number of people in the next two millennia. James, the Lord's brother, had an even greater surprise. In Jesus' lifetime, he was the classic sceptic. He and his brothers wanted to lock Jesus up as 'out of his mind' (see Mark 3:20–22); they did not believe in Jesus (John 7:5) – and yet after the ascension, they are found in prayer with Mary and the Apostles (Acts 1:14). James is described as the effective chairman of the Council of Jerusalem (Acts15:13), and the Jewish historian Josephus, writing at the end of the first century, records the martyrdom of James in AD 61. How did this transformation come about? The explanation of this extraordinary turn-around is given by Paul, writing about AD 55, with simple and graphic words:

Then he appeared to James, then to all the apostles, and last of all he appeared to me also, as to one abnormally born.

(1 Corinthians 15:7–8)

The conversion of James is recorded in Scripture, and also in Jewish secular history by Josephus. The transformation of the apostolic group, and the rather braver and more faithful women, is equally remarkable. On the evening of Good Friday, one was about to commit suicide, another was broken by his denial, and the rest were hiding behind locked doors. Jesus' burial was accomplished by two secret disciples, Joseph of Arimathea and Nicodemus (see chapter 1), and his body anointed by a faithful group of women. No one was expecting a good outcome. The women who came to the tomb were astonished, perplexed, and filled with holy fear. In a moment we will read John's account of that first Easter morning. And if we take the evidence seriously, we must respond. If the Easter story is true, then it is worse than useless, in the language of the opening chapter, for us to remain as spiritual caterpillars. Many of you reading this will know that this is a choice that you have already made; some of you will not yet be ready, you have begun a journey of enquiry but are still living with too many questions; a few of you may wonder how you could take such a step. The prayer that follows is just one of many different ways of responding. You might want to pray like this for yourself (either on your own or with some experienced believer):

Photo 6: Blue-spotted Charaxes (wingspan 95mm) similar to those flying in trees in Mutwe Wa Nkoko. Photo lifesize

A prayer
of response

Lord, I realise that you have cared for me and known me long before I was born. Lord, I know that I have acted selfishly. I have sinned against heaven and against you. Thank you Lord, that you bore my sins in your body on the tree, that I might die to sin and live for righteousness. Lord, you promised the gift of the Holy Spirit to those who ask in faith, I believe that you rose from the dead, and I acknowledge you as Lord and Saviour. Lord, help me to truly repent, to receive the gift of the Holy Spirit and of new life in Christ Jesus.

This prayer is illustrated by the photographic sequence on this page and the next. It is based on Psalm 139:13–16, Luke 15:18, 1 Peter 2:24, Luke 11:13, Romans 10:9 and 2 Corinthians 5:14–21.

The sequence of photographs shows the life cycle of the Purple Emperor from the egg laid on sallow in late July, through the caterpillar stage from autumn to spring, pupation takes place under a sallow leaf in June, and the butterflies fly mainly in July. Only the males have the iridescent purple sheen. (Egg height 1mm; small caterpillars, 3mm, 7mm, 9mm; full size caterpillar 42mm; chrysalis 30mm; male butterfly wingspan 75mm, female 84mm. Note the camouflage shown by the change of colouring in the hibernating caterpillar and in the one about to pupate.)

If you have made such a prayer for the first time, you are like a newborn butterfly (see chapter 2). You will need to trust that 'He who began a good work in you will carry it on to completion' (Philippians 1:6). You will need the help of other Christians – you are part of the body of the church (1 Corinthians 12:12–14). Unlike the newly emerged butterfly, you will have many new friends! More than that, the risen Christ, himself, has promised to be with you.

> *Therefore go and make disciples of all nations, baptising them in the name of the Father, and of the Son, and of the Holy Spirit, and teaching them to obey everything I have commanded you. And surely I am with you always, to the very end of the age.*
>
> (Matthew 28:19–20)

> *Early on the first day of the week, while it was still dark, Mary Magdalene went to the tomb and saw that the stone had been removed from the entrance. So she came running to Simon Peter and the other disciple, the one Jesus loved, and said, 'They have taken the Lord out of the tomb, and we don't know where they have put him!'*
>
> *So Peter and the other disciple started for the tomb. Both were running, but the other disciple outran Peter and reached the tomb first. He bent over and looked in at the strips of linen lying there but did not go in. Then Simon Peter, who was behind him, arrived and went into the tomb. He saw the strips of linen lying there, as well as the burial cloth that had been around Jesus' head. The cloth was folded up by itself, separate from the linen. Finally, the other disciple, who had reached the tomb first, also went inside. He saw and believed. (They still did not understand from Scripture that Jesus had to rise from the dead.)*
>
> *Then the disciples went back to their homes, but Mary stood outside the tomb crying. As she wept, she bent over to look into the tomb and saw two angels in white, seated where Jesus' body had been, one at the head and the other at the foot.*
>
> *They asked her, 'Woman why are you crying?'*
>
> *'They have taken my Lord away,' she said, 'and I don't know where they have put him.' At this she turned round and*

Photo 7: The folded grave clothes, and the empty tomb, described so eloquently by St John are illustrated here by a sunlit empty chrysalis.

saw Jesus standing there, but she did not realise that it was Jesus.

'Woman,' he said, 'Why are you crying? Who is it you are looking for?' Thinking he was the gardener, she said, 'Sir, if you have carried him away, tell me where you have put him, and I will get him.'

Jesus said to her, 'Mary.' She turned towards him and cried out in Aramaic, 'Rabboni' (which means Teacher).

Jesus said, 'Do not hold onto me, for I have not yet returned to my Father. Go instead to my brothers and tell them, "I am returning to my Father and your Father, to my God and your God."'

Mary Magdalene went to the disciples with the news: 'I have seen the Lord!' And she told them that he had said these things to her.

(John 20:1–18)

Notes

1. John Woolmer, *Angels* (Monarch, 2003), chapter 7.
2. *Ibid*, chapter 1.